T0354047

ADVOCATE

A GRAPHIC MEMOIR OF FAMILY, COMMUNITY, AND THE FIGHT FOR ENVIRONMENTAL JUSTICE

ADVOCATE

EDDIE AHN

TEN SPEED GRAPHIC
An imprint of TEN SPEED PRESS
California | New York

CONTENTS

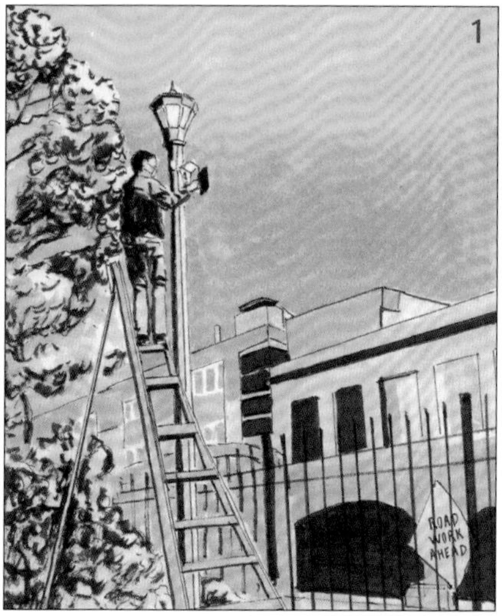
1
ROAD WORK AHEAD

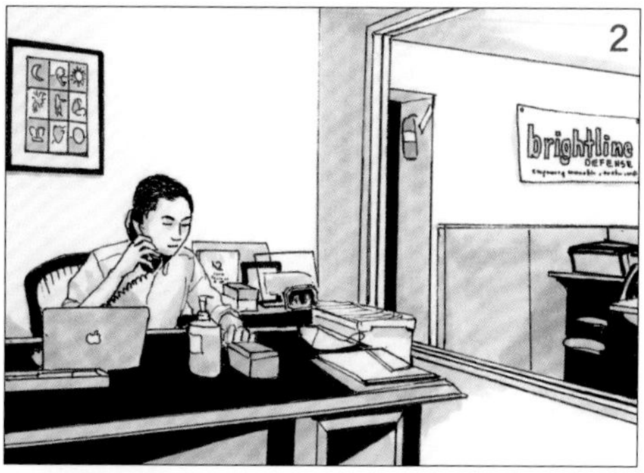
2
brightline
DEFENSE

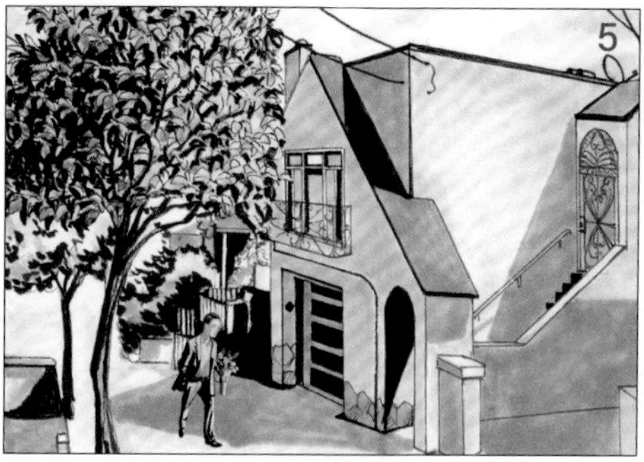
5

SCENE LOCATIONS

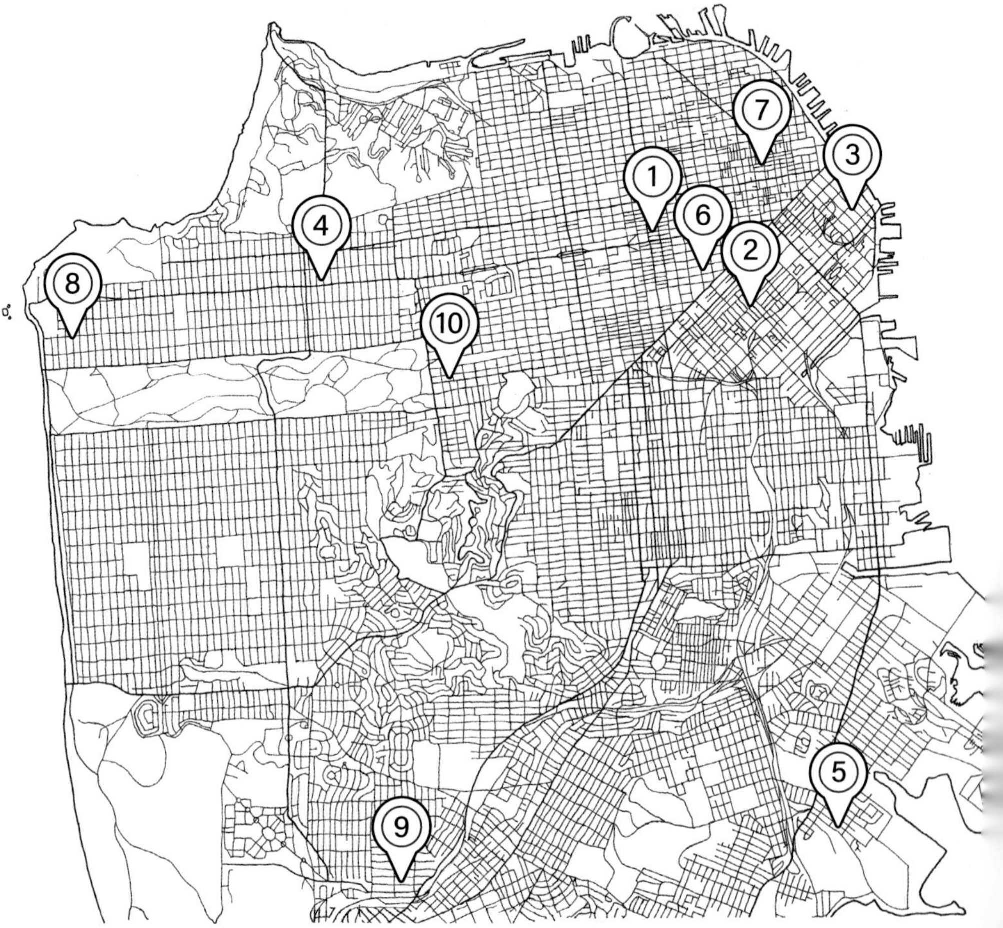
7
3
1
6
2
4
8
10
5
9

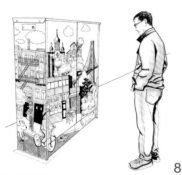

LOCATIONS

1. Macaulay Park (Tenderloin)
2. Brightline's Office (South of Market)
3. The Bay Area Metro Center (Headquarters to several regional government agencies)
4. Geary Parkway Motel (Inner Richmond District)
5. Dr. Espanola Jackson's Home (Bayview–Hunters Point)
6. UC College of the Law, San Francisco (formerly University of California, Hastings College of the Law) (Tenderloin)
7. Chinatown
8. Box Art (There are 10 of these! This one is in the Outer Richmond.)
9. Oceanview
10. The Alembic (Great bar in the Haight)

PROLOGUE

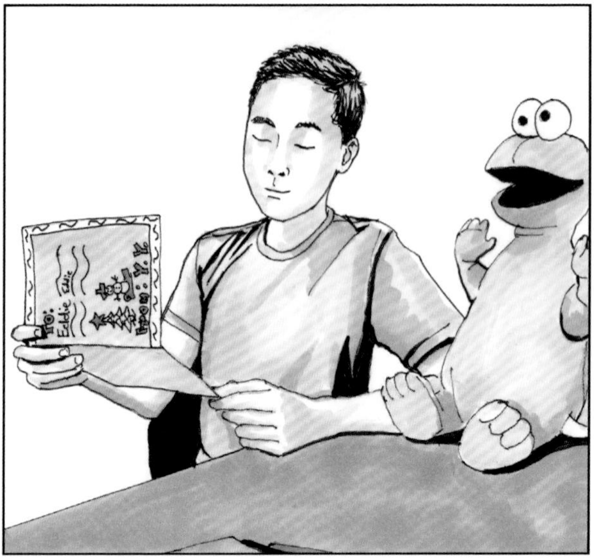
Eddie
From: Y.K.

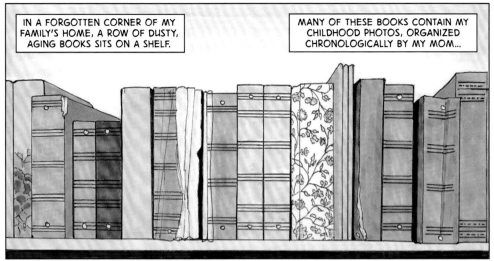

IN A FORGOTTEN CORNER OF MY FAMILY'S HOME, A ROW OF DUSTY, AGING BOOKS SITS ON A SHELF.

MANY OF THESE BOOKS CONTAIN MY CHILDHOOD PHOTOS, ORGANIZED CHRONOLOGICALLY BY MY MOM...

...BUT EVEN NEATLY SEQUENCED, THESE PHOTO ALBUMS DON'T REVEAL MUCH.

Eddie 4

AS I LOOK AT PHOTOS OF MYSELF IN OUR FAMILY'S STORE, IT'S HARD TO PINPOINT WHAT LED TO MY CAREER IN ENVIRONMENTAL JUSTICE.

I FIND MUCH OLDER FAMILY PHOTOS, JUMBLED TOGETHER IN A BAG...

...IF MY OWN PHOTOS CAN'T PROVIDE ANSWERS, THEN MAYBE I NEED TO LOOK EVEN FURTHER BACK TO THE PAST.

1954

MY GRANDPARENTS MARRIED AFTER THE END OF THE KOREAN WAR.

MY GRANDFATHER HAD SERVED AS A TRANSLATOR, AND U.S. MILITARY OFFICIALS ATTENDED THEIR WEDDING.

A PROUD INTELLECTUAL WHO BELIEVED IN HIS SERVICE, HE HAD SURVIVED MANY TRAGEDIES DURING THE WAR.

POST-WAR KOREA

North Korea

Kaesong

Seoul

South Korea

HIS HOMETOWN, KAESONG (개성), WAS THE ONLY CITY TO PERMANENTLY CHANGE CONTROL FROM SOUTH KOREA TO NORTH KOREA.

HE WAS 21 AND HAD BEEN STUDYING IN SEOUL, SOUTH KOREA'S CAPITAL, WHEN THE WAR BROKE OUT. FOR OVER *FIVE DECADES*, HE NEVER HEARD FROM HIS FAMILY IN KAESONG AGAIN.

HE PASSED AWAY IN 2005, AND ALL THAT REMAINS OF HIM ARE A FEW PHOTOS AND SOME PAPERS FILLED WITH HIS THOUGHTS, SCRIBBLED IN PENCIL.

DESPITE WHAT I'VE LEARNED THROUGH FAMILY RETELLINGS, HIS WRITINGS DON'T REVEAL TOO MUCH ABOUT HIS FEELINGS, CAREER, OR GENERATION'S STRUGGLES...

...ALTHOUGH IT'S NOT FROM A LACK OF ATTENTION TO DETAIL.

I FIND BRIEF NOTES ABOUT DAILY MEALS AND PURCHASES AT THE BOOKSTORE.

HE HAD EVEN METICULOUSLY CORRECTED DAYS AND DATES FOR 2003 ENTRIES...

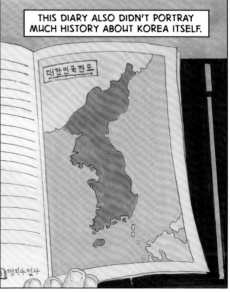

...IN AN OLD DIARY DESIGNED FOR THE YEAR 1990.

THIS DIARY ALSO DIDN'T PORTRAY MUCH HISTORY ABOUT KOREA ITSELF.

13

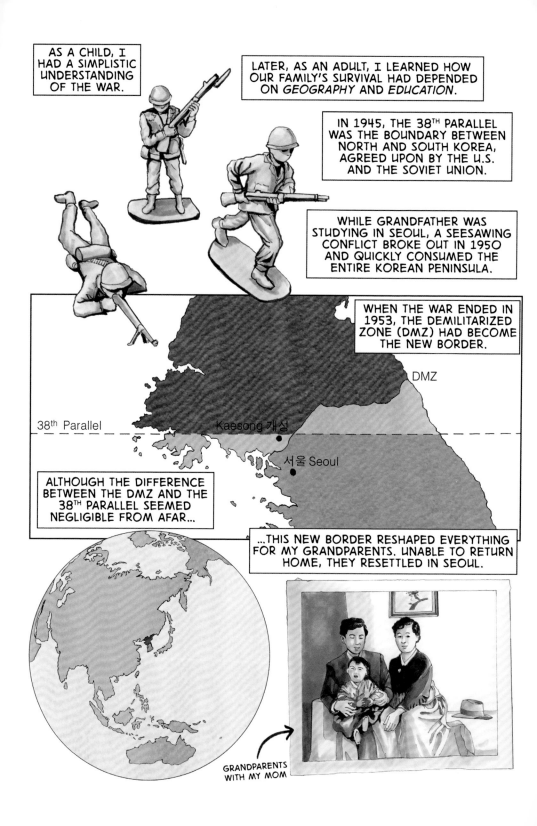

AS A CHILD, I HAD A SIMPLISTIC UNDERSTANDING OF THE WAR.

LATER, AS AN ADULT, I LEARNED HOW OUR FAMILY'S SURVIVAL HAD DEPENDED ON *GEOGRAPHY* AND *EDUCATION*.

IN 1945, THE 38TH PARALLEL WAS THE BOUNDARY BETWEEN NORTH AND SOUTH KOREA, AGREED UPON BY THE U.S. AND THE SOVIET UNION.

WHILE GRANDFATHER WAS STUDYING IN SEOUL, A SEESAWING CONFLICT BROKE OUT IN 1950 AND QUICKLY CONSUMED THE ENTIRE KOREAN PENINSULA.

WHEN THE WAR ENDED IN 1953, THE DEMILITARIZED ZONE (DMZ) HAD BECOME THE NEW BORDER.

DMZ

38th Parallel

Kaesong 개성

서울 Seoul

ALTHOUGH THE DIFFERENCE BETWEEN THE DMZ AND THE 38TH PARALLEL SEEMED NEGLIGIBLE FROM AFAR...

...THIS NEW BORDER RESHAPED EVERYTHING FOR MY GRANDPARENTS. UNABLE TO RETURN HOME, THEY RESETTLED IN SEOUL.

GRANDPARENTS WITH MY MOM

14

GEOGRAPHY AND EDUCATION SHAPED OUR FAMILY'S IMMIGRATION HISTORY IN THE U.S. TOO.

IN 1980, MY PARENTS CAME TO THE U.S. FOR GRADUATE SCHOOL.

MY MOM TRAINED TO BE A PHARMACIST, AND MY DAD STUDIED ENGINEERING.

THERE WAS AN OPPORTUNITY FOR MY MOM TO GO TO SCHOOL IN CALIFORNIA, BUT FINANCES AND THE TIMING OF THEIR MARRIAGE LED THEM TO BOTH ENROLL IN THE UNIVERSITY OF TEXAS AT AUSTIN.

DURING THEIR STUDIES, I WAS BORN IN AUSTIN. MY SISTER WAS BORN THREE YEARS LATER...

...AND BY 1988, MOTIVATED TO MAKE MONEY MORE QUICKLY THAN WHAT THEIR DEGREES ALLOWED, MY PARENTS STARTED THEIR FIRST STORE.

15

OVER TIME, MY OWN JOURNEY WOULD BE LARGELY DEFINED BY MY NONPROFIT WORK OUT WEST...

...BUILT ON A HIGHER EDUCATION DEGREE FROM THE NORTHEAST...

...AS WELL AS THE FAMILY BUSINESS AND HISTORY FROM DOWN SOUTH.

AS I TURN BACK TO MY OWN KEEPSAKES, I FIND ANOTHER DUSTY COLLECTION OF MY HISTORY.

IT'S FILLED WITH RANDOM GIFTS AND NOTES FROM ELEMENTARY STUDENTS, ADDRESSED TO ME.

THEIR NOTES FEEL LIKE THEY'RE FROM A *LIFETIME* AGO...

...SO MUCH HAS HAPPENED SINCE THEN.

WHILE MY GRANDFATHER'S PAPERS MARKED THE END OF HIS LIFE AND STORY, THESE NOTES AND LETTERS ARE WHERE MY OWN STORY BEGINS.

A STORY THAT SPANS OVER 15 YEARS OF NONPROFIT WORK AND SHARING COMMUNITY.

CHAPTER ONE

COME BACK
SOON

IN 2005, I JOINED AMERICORPS AS A WORKER FOR AN AFTERSCHOOL PROGRAM IN OAKLAND CHINATOWN. INSPIRED BY MY FINAL COLLEGE CLASS ON EDUCATION POLICY, I WAS KEEN TO WORK FOR A PROGRAM THAT SUPPORTED IMMIGRANT FAMILIES AND YOUTH.

YOUTH OF THE PROGRAM WOULD WRITE ALL THEIR OBSERVATIONS ABOUT ME:

Eddie

Eddie is my Blue Group leader. He is very nice and funny. Eddie likes to put his hands on top of his head and he is very good at four-square.

IN ADDITION TO BEING GOOD AT FOUR-SQUARE, I TAUGHT ART AND PUBLIC SPEAKING WORKSHOPS.

When Eddie talks, he gestures. Eddie has a reddish nose like Rudolph. Eddie's pants doesn't have holes like other tutors.

I ALSO LED HOMEWORK TUTORIAL SESSIONS, PAIRING ELEMENTARY SCHOOL STUDENTS WITH VOLUNTEERS FROM UC BERKELEY, WHO DRESSED MORE FASHIONABLY.

MY DAYS WERE FULL OF JOY AND JOKES WITH THE YOUTH...

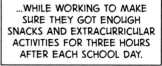

Eddie likes to smile, and he likes to take away Jenny chips, but he can't. Eddie is a cool leader.

...WHILE WORKING TO MAKE SURE THEY GOT ENOUGH SNACKS AND EXTRACURRICULAR ACTIVITIES FOR THREE HOURS AFTER EACH SCHOOL DAY.

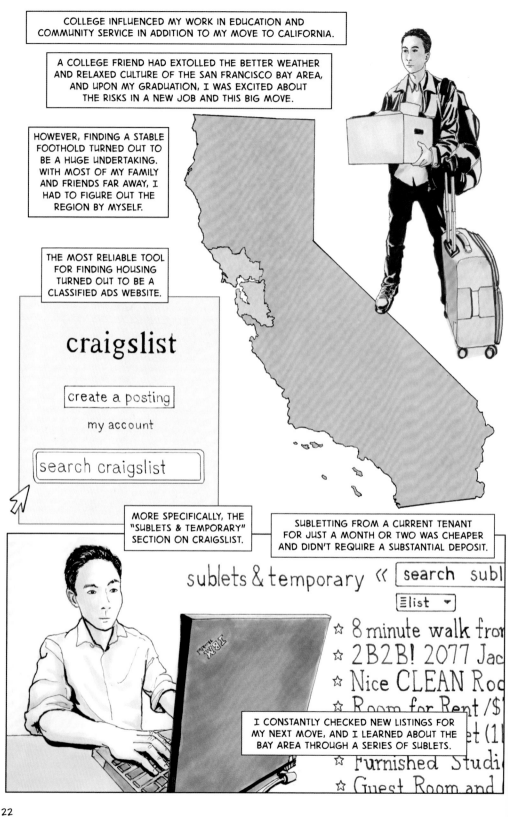

COLLEGE INFLUENCED MY WORK IN EDUCATION AND COMMUNITY SERVICE IN ADDITION TO MY MOVE TO CALIFORNIA.

A COLLEGE FRIEND HAD EXTOLLED THE BETTER WEATHER AND RELAXED CULTURE OF THE SAN FRANCISCO BAY AREA, AND UPON MY GRADUATION, I WAS EXCITED ABOUT THE RISKS IN A NEW JOB AND THIS BIG MOVE.

HOWEVER, FINDING A STABLE FOOTHOLD TURNED OUT TO BE A HUGE UNDERTAKING. WITH MOST OF MY FAMILY AND FRIENDS FAR AWAY, I HAD TO FIGURE OUT THE REGION BY MYSELF.

THE MOST RELIABLE TOOL FOR FINDING HOUSING TURNED OUT TO BE A CLASSIFIED ADS WEBSITE.

craigslist

create a posting

my account

search craigslist

MORE SPECIFICALLY, THE "SUBLETS & TEMPORARY" SECTION ON CRAIGSLIST.

SUBLETTING FROM A CURRENT TENANT FOR JUST A MONTH OR TWO WAS CHEAPER AND DIDN'T REQUIRE A SUBSTANTIAL DEPOSIT.

sublets & temporary « search subl

list ▼

☆ 8 minute walk from
☆ 2B2B! 2077 Jac
☆ Nice CLEAN Roc
☆ Room for Rent /$

I CONSTANTLY CHECKED NEW LISTINGS FOR MY NEXT MOVE, AND I LEARNED ABOUT THE BAY AREA THROUGH A SERIES OF SUBLETS.

☆ Furnished Studi
☆ Guest Room and

NEAR ONE SUBLET, I GOT TO EAT A BURRITO OF A SIZE TYPICAL OF THE BAY AREA.

cactus

HUH.

I'M PROBABLY GONNA PASS OUT AFTER EATING THIS MUCH FOOD...

THESE BURRITOS WOULD LATER TURN OUT TO BE *ESSENTIAL* TO MY DIET.

AT ANOTHER SUBLET IN OAKLAND, I LIVED IN A RUN-DOWN HOUSE WHERE VEGETABLES WERE GROWN IN ROCKY SOIL AND BROKEN CONCRETE.

THE VEGETABLES WERE THEN MADE INTO A SOUP AND EATEN BY TENANTS OF THE HOUSE.

MY MOST INTERESTING SUBLETTING EXPERIENCE WAS IN OAKLAND CHINATOWN.

THE TENANT WAS A MASSAGE THERAPIST WHO WORKED IN THE APARTMENT. IN A TOUR OF THE PLACE, I WAS LED DOWN A DIMLY LIT HALLWAY.

A CURTAIN SEPARATED THE HALLWAY FROM AN EVEN DARKER ROOM.

I WASN'T QUITE PREPARED FOR WHAT CAME NEXT.

THE ROOM'S FLOOR WAS LINED WITH MATTRESSES THAT SOFTLY CREAKED UNDER MY FEET AS HE PROCLAIMED:

WELCOME TO *THE WOMB!*

IN HINDSIGHT, THIS SHOULD HAVE RAISED MORE FLAGS FOR WHAT WAS TO COME.

SO MY ROOM IS $500, IN CASH?

YEP!

BUT I WAS FOCUSED MORE ON *PRICE* AND THE *SHORT COMMUTE* TO THE SCHOOL.

23

UNTIL THAT POINT, THE LENGTH OF MY COMMUTE HAD BEEN SHAPED BY PUBLIC TRANSIT.

STARTING WITH THE TRAINS OF BART (BAY AREA RAPID TRANSIT).

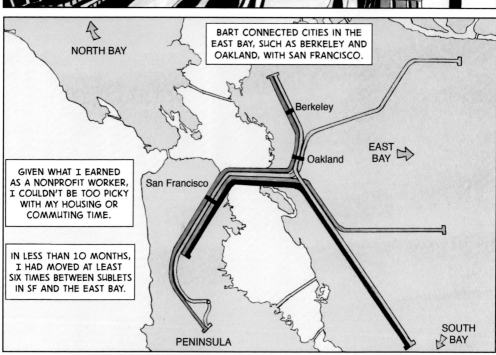

NORTH BAY

BART CONNECTED CITIES IN THE EAST BAY, SUCH AS BERKELEY AND OAKLAND, WITH SAN FRANCISCO.

Berkeley

Oakland

EAST BAY

San Francisco

GIVEN WHAT I EARNED AS A NONPROFIT WORKER, I COULDN'T BE TOO PICKY WITH MY HOUSING OR COMMUTING TIME.

IN LESS THAN 10 MONTHS, I HAD MOVED AT LEAST SIX TIMES BETWEEN SUBLETS IN SF AND THE EAST BAY.

PENINSULA

SOUTH BAY

WITH BART, MOVING AROUND WAS EASY ENOUGH, AS ALL MY STUFF COULD FIT IN A BOX AND TWO BAGS.

I ALSO BECAME FAMILIAR WITH THE BUSES OF SF MUNI AND AC TRANSIT, READING OR SLEEPING DURING THE LONG COMMUTES.

Z

MY COMMUTE USED TO BE OVER 90 MINUTES, BUT FROM THE OAKLAND CHINATOWN SUBLET, I COULD NOW WALK TO WORK IN **5** MINUTES.

ON MY WALK HOME, IT WAS ALSO FUN TO OCCASIONALLY SEE THE YOUTH AND FAMILIES I SERVED.

HEY, EDDIE GUERRERO!

AT FIRST, I DIDN'T THINK MUCH OF MY ROOMMATE RUNNING A MASSAGE BUSINESS OUT OF THE APARTMENT.

EVERYTHING ABOUT THE PLACE EXUDED QUIRKY, SOOTHING *NEW AGE* VIBES.

MY ROOM WAS DOWN THE HALLWAY, AND I LIKED ITS SPARSE FURNISHINGS.

WITH MY ROOMMATE TRAVELING FOR THE FIRST MONTH, I ALSO HAD PEACE AND QUIET TO DO A LOT OF READING AND DRAWING.

BUT ONCE MY ROOMMATE RETURNED AND STARTED BRINGING CLIENTS TO THE APARTMENT, SOUND TRAVELED THROUGH THE THIN WALLS...

Ooh!

OH! mmm... uhhh...OH YES!

...AND I QUICKLY FOUND OUT THE CLIENTS WERE **NOT** GETTING A SHIATSU OR SWEDISH MASSAGE.

OH! huh... YES! huhhh OH!!

INCREDIBLY, MY ROOMMATE'S STAMINA FOR SERVICING CLIENTS LASTED BOTH DAY *AND* NIGHT.

MY STUDENTS, EVER THE KEEN OBSERVERS, POINTED OUT MY HAGGARD APPEARANCE FROM A LACK OF SLEEP.

WHY ARE YOU LOOKING SO TIRED, EDDIE!

UH, I WAS PLAYING A COMPUTER GAME REALLY LATE...

I MADE UP A FEEBLE EXCUSE, *ANYTHING* TO AVOID TELLING YOUTH ABOUT THIS ISSUE...

...*ESPECIALLY* WHEN THERE WERE OTHER CRISES TO ADDRESS.

ON ONE OCCASION, A TYPICALLY HAPPY-GO-LUCKY 5TH GRADER BECAME FRUSTRATED DURING A HOMEWORK TUTORIAL SESSION.

I TRIED THE USUAL INSTRUCTION STEPS...

OK, LET'S TAKE THIS A LITTLE BIT AT A TIME.

SO HOW MANY WHOLE GROUPS OF TWO CAN WE PULL OUT OF FIVE?

...BUT THERE WASN'T ANY THOUGHT AND RESPONSE.

INSTEAD, SILENT TEARS BEGAN ROLLING DOWN HIS FACE AS HE SHOOK HIS HEAD FITFULLY.

AS IF HAVING A MIND OF ITS OWN, THE PENCIL TWITCHED IN HIS CLENCHED FIST.

WITH HIS CLASSMATES ALL AROUND US, I KNEW PRESSING ON WITH LONG DIVISION WOULD ACCELERATE A PUBLIC MELTDOWN.

ANOTHER TACK WAS NECESSARY.

ALRIGHT, LET'S TAKE A QUICK BREAK.

MY OWN GROWTH AS A SELF-TAUGHT ARTIST WAS *SLOW*, AND I COULD DOODLE ONLY A HANDFUL OF THINGS.

WOULD YOU LIKE TO DRAW?

NO, *YOU* DRAW.

SO I DIDN'T OFTEN DRAW ON DEMAND FOR THE YOUTH...

...BUT I WOULD MAKE AN EXCEPTION THIS TIME.

OK, WHAT WOULD YOU LIKE?

...HORSE.

HM, THAT'S A *TOUGH* ONE, BUT I CAN WALK YOU THROUGH IT.

I BELIEVED THAT MY STUDENTS SHOULD CREATE AND FIGURE OUT ART FOR THEMSELVES.

SO YOU CAN SEE THE BACK *CURVE* A BIT...

ON THE OTHER HAND, A PROPER HORSE DRAWING WASN'T PARTICULARLY IMPORTANT, NO MORE THAN CALCULATING THE QUOTIENT IN A MATH PROBLEM.

AS LONG AS HIS JOY AND INGENUITY WERE PRESERVED FOR ANOTHER DAY, I WOULD TAKE THAT AS A SMALL WIN.

...HOW ABOUT SOME WINGS ON THE HORSE?

YES.

HIS TEARS SUBSIDED AS WE WORKED THROUGH THE DRAWING TOGETHER.

GENERALLY, WORKING WITH YOUTH REQUIRED A LOT OF PATIENCE.

THEY WOULD OBSESS OVER WHICH CLASS HAD MORE RECREATION TIME AND WROTE ABSOLUTIST LETTERS ABOUT ITS FAIRNESS.

Dear Eddie,
How come your color group gets to play games? It is so very unfair! Write back why tomorrow.

It's not fair!

TO SHAME ON you Eddie FROM SHAME on you

you are a super excellent group

n is homework time some and get game and get to play why is they get to play we don't good about them, they finish their they can play Game and we don't

I DIDN'T TAKE THESE DEMANDS TOO SERIOUSLY. THE STUDENTS KNEW THEY WERE TESTING LIMITS, AND SOME WOULD OCCASIONALLY WRITE KNOWING LETTERS.

You 〔Hi!〕〔Hi!〕Me

Dear Eddie,
    I like your drawings and you are very fair. I knew when you grew a little older you would be a great artist. Do you like my drawings? I hope you do. You are almost like Santa Claus, you are very kind and helpful. I hope that you can write a letter back to me some day.

BESIDES ART WORKSHOPS, I ALSO TAUGHT A PUBLIC SPEAKING CLASS FOR 3RD THROUGH 5TH GRADERS.

PREPARATION WAS EASY ENOUGH...

OK, WE WATCHED THE MOVIE *SPIRITED AWAY* LAST WEEK...

AND NOW, YOU'VE WRITTEN A SHORT SPEECH ON *WHY* YOU LIKE IT.

SO WHO WANTS TO GO FIRST?!

...BUT WHEN IT WAS TIME TO VOLUNTEER FOR SPEAKING IN FRONT OF EVERYONE, IT WENT ABOUT AS WELL AS YOU COULD EXPECT.

...

C'MON, ANYONE??

I ENJOYED THE CREATIVITY IN TRYING TO DRAW OUT THEIR BEST.

ALRIGHT, ERIC! YOU HAVE TO GET THROUGH *THREE REASONS* IN *TWO MINUTES!*

ESPECIALLY FROM THE GROUCHIEST STUDENTS.

AW, *MAN.*

DO I *HAVE* TO? I'M *HECKA* BORED.

THAT'S WHY YOU GOTTA GO *NOW!*

YOU HAVE TO GET THROUGH YOUR SPEECH *WITHOUT* LAUGHING, OK?

TO DO SO, I WOULD THROW IN MORE CHALLENGES THEIR WAY.

WELL, *SPIRITED AWAY* IS THE BEST MOVIE BECAUSE, *ONE*, IT GOT A DRAGON IN IT...

hehe

...AND *TWO*, THE MAIN CHARACTER GETS TO RIDE AROUND ON THE DRAGON...

...AND THAT WAS REALLY COOL.

hehe
hehe
haha

IT WASN'T SUPER IMPORTANT *WHAT* THE STUDENTS SAID, OR EVEN *HOW* THEY SAID IT.

THE GOAL WASN'T TO SUDDENLY TRANSFORM THEM INTO ORATORS LIKE JFK OR MALCOLM X.

AND THIRD, I... I GUESS...

haha
hehehe
HEH

I LIKE THE MONSTER *NO-FACE* AND HOW...*HEH*--

HEHEHE
HAHAHA

REMEMBER, *NO* LAUGHING! OR YOU GOTTA START OVER AGAIN.

OK, *OK.* THE CHARACTER IS BOTH GOOD AND BAD...

ALL THIS WAS FOR SOMETHING MORE FUNDAMENTAL: TO *NOT* FEAR OR DREAD SPEAKING IN FRONT OF AN AUDIENCE.

AND MORE THAN ANYTHING, TO BE ABLE TO EXPRESS ONESELF.

HAHAHA
HAHAHA
HEHEHE
HEHEHE

FOR THIS END, *LOOKING SILLY* WAS WORTH IT.

AT HOME, I TRIED USING OTHER DISTRACTIONS LIKE MUSIC WITH LIMITED SUCCESS.

BUT BECAUSE OF THIS TUMULT, I LEARNED HOW TO CAREFULLY MEASURE RESPONSES TO SURPRISING MOMENTS AT WORK.

ONE PARTICULAR STUDENT DEMANDED *A LOT* OF ATTENTION, WHICH I USUALLY DIDN'T MIND.

MORE WORRISOME WAS WHEN THIS STUDENT'S EARNEST EXPRESSIONS VEERED INTO MUCH DARKER TERRITORY.

AS WITH HURRICANE KATRINA, NEWS AND POP CULTURE OFTEN CAME UP IN THE CLASSROOM AND ON THE PLAYGROUND.

MANY OF MY STUDENTS WERE AVID FANS OF PROFESSIONAL WRESTLING, AND THEY GOT A KICK OUT OF ADDRESSING ME AS THE PRO WRESTLER THEY KNEW FROM WATCHING TV:

WHEN EDDIE GUERRERO SUDDENLY DIED IN LATE 2005, THEIR GREETING WAS MORE SUBDUED.

HEY, EDDIE GUERRERO. YOU *DIED* TODAY.

THIS LIMITED CULTURAL FRAME OF REFERENCE ALSO WENT BEYOND MY FIRST NAME.

PRIOR TO THE RISE OF K-POP AND DRAMAS, MANY STUDENTS IN OAKLAND CHINATOWN DIDN'T KNOW MUCH ABOUT KOREA.

FOR INSTANCE, WHEN I TOLD ONE STUDENT MY FAVORITE FOOD WAS KOREAN BBQ...

...SHE WROTE:

Eddie likes to eat cream barbacue, and sometimes burns his hands on the barbacue grill.

IMAGINING ICE CREAM ON A GRILL AMUSED ME ENDLESSLY.

I WONDER IF MY GRANDFATHER WOULD HAVE RELATED TO MY EARLY YEARS.

HE HAD GRADUATED FROM SEOUL NATIONAL UNIVERSITY, SOUTH KOREA'S MOST PRESTIGIOUS ACADEMIC INSTITUTION, AND HE COULD BE DIFFICULT AND DISTANT.

STILL, I ENJOYED TALKING AND LEARNING FROM HIM WHEN I VISITED SEOUL EVERY FEW YEARS.

JUST A YEAR BEFORE I STARTED LIVING IN OAKLAND CHINATOWN, HE PASSED AWAY, AND GIVEN HIS HIGH EDUCATIONAL STANDARDS, I PROBABLY WOULD HAVE STRUGGLED TO EXPLAIN MY WORK WITH YOUTH...

...AS I DID WITH MY MOM.

<IF THIS NOTE WAS WRITTEN BY A 5TH GRADER, WHY IS THE SPELLING WRONG?>

UMMA!

MOST OF MY STUDENTS COME FROM FAMILIES THAT DON'T SPEAK ENGLISH.

I THOUGHT MY MOM WOULD APPRECIATE THE VALUE OF SERVING IMMIGRANT FAMILIES WITHOUT THE MEANS TO PROVIDE THE BEST EDUCATION FOR THEIR CHILDREN.

IT'S ABOUT THE *COMMUNITY* GETTING A BETTER EDUCATION.

THE YOUTH GET INDIVIDUAL TUTORING AND EXTRACURRICULAR ACTIVITIES LIKE ARTS AND SPORTS.

THEIR FAMILIES DON'T HAVE A LOT OF RESOURCES AND MAKE LESS THAN $20,000 A YEAR.

UNFORTUNATELY, OUR CIRCULAR DISCUSSIONS ABOUT NONPROFIT WORK OFTEN FOCUSED ON A *DIFFERENT* VALUE.

BUT HOW MUCH DO *YOU* GET PAID?

THIS ENDLESS DANCE TO EXPLAIN MY NONPROFIT WORK WAS SHAPED BY OUR FAMILY'S BUSINESS AND ITS DETAILS.

WHERE EVERY BOTTLE WAS DEFINED BY A PRICE TAG AND SUBSEQUENT TRANSACTION.

FOR OVER 20 YEARS, THE BACKBONE OF THE FAMILY BUSINESS WAS LIQUOR RETAIL.

SO FROM AN EARLY AGE, I WAS SURROUNDED BY A *WORLD* OF TRANSACTIONS.

COLONY BOTTLE SHOP (CBS) WAS THE FIRST FAMILY STORE, ESTABLISHED IN THE COLONY, A SUBURB OF DALLAS, TEXAS.

WHEN THE BUSINESS MOVED OUT OF THE COLONY, THE SIGNAGE "CBS" WAS KEPT.

"*COLD BEER STORE*" WAS CREATED AS A BACKRONYM.

MY EARLIEST MEMORIES ARE OF INVENTORY COMING AND GOING.

UNLOADING BOTTLES FROM BOXES ONTO SHELVES...AND THEN REUSING EMPTY BOXES TO PACK UP LARGE PURCHASE ORDERS FOR CUSTOMERS.

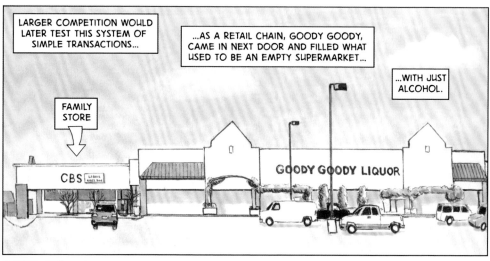

LARGER COMPETITION WOULD LATER TEST THIS SYSTEM OF SIMPLE TRANSACTIONS...

...AS A RETAIL CHAIN, GOODY GOODY, CAME IN NEXT DOOR AND FILLED WHAT USED TO BE AN EMPTY SUPERMARKET...

...WITH JUST ALCOHOL.

FAMILY STORE

WE WORKED TO DISTINGUISH OURSELVES WITH CUSTOMER SERVICE AND MARKETING.

THE STORE'S SIGNAGE WAS REPURPOSED AS A CATCHIER BACKRONYM.

SO "CBS" BECAME:

COME BACK SOON!

EVEN AGAINST BAD ODDS, MY DAD SEEMED TO ALWAYS WORK WITH CHEER AND CREATIVITY.

JUST ACROSS FROM THE ELEMENTARY SCHOOL IN OAKLAND, THE CORNER STORE WAS A DAILY REMINDER OF MY OWN CHILDHOOD.

JENNY, YOU **KNOW** PROGRAM RULES!

YOU CAN'T TAKE CHIPS TO CLASS.

NYAH!

I COULD'VE BEEN MORE DRACONIAN, BUT I WAS SOFTENED BY MY MEMORIES OF TREATS FROM MY FAMILY'S STORE.

PARTICULARLY THE SPECIAL OCCASION OF A SODA CAN, SELECTED FROM SO MANY FLAVORS AND FESTIVE LABELS.

HEE! HEE!

WHILE HANGING OUT IN THE BEER FREEZER, I WOULD SAVOR THIS SINGLE CAN.

RRRRRRRR

THE EXTREME COLD AND LOUD ROAR OF THE FANS ADDED TO THE EXCITEMENT AND SUGAR HIGH.

POSTER ADS IN THE LIQUOR STORE TRANSPORTED ME TO EXOTIC LOCATIONS AND LIMITLESS LIFESTYLES...

Anything can happen.

sip!

...SOMETIMES MAKING ME FORGET THEY WERE JUST BOTTLES ON A SHELF.

1999

35

DESPITE THE ORDINARY MERCHANDISE, MY DAD SEEMED PROUD OF HAVING HIS OWN BUSINESS, SINCE HE HADN'T ENJOYED HIS PREVIOUS ENGINEERING JOB.

THE STORE ITSELF REPRESENTED PROGRESS, AND WE RECEIVED A LOT OF MARKETING NOVELTIES THAT SYMBOLIZED OUR ECONOMIC MOBILITY...

...SUCH AS A TOY TRAIN OR HOT AIR BALLOON RIDE PROMOTING WHISKEY...

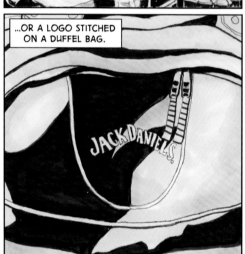

...OR A LOGO STITCHED ON A DUFFEL BAG.

FROM SUBLET TO SUBLET, I CARRIED MY STUFF WRAPPED IN THIS HISTORY...

A CONSTANT REMINDER OF HOW MY PARENTS PLANNED FOR OUR FAMILY'S SUCCESS.

THE PATH *UPWARD* WOULD BE SOMETHING LIKE THIS:

STUDY HARD AND GO TO A RESPECTABLE UNIVERSITY...

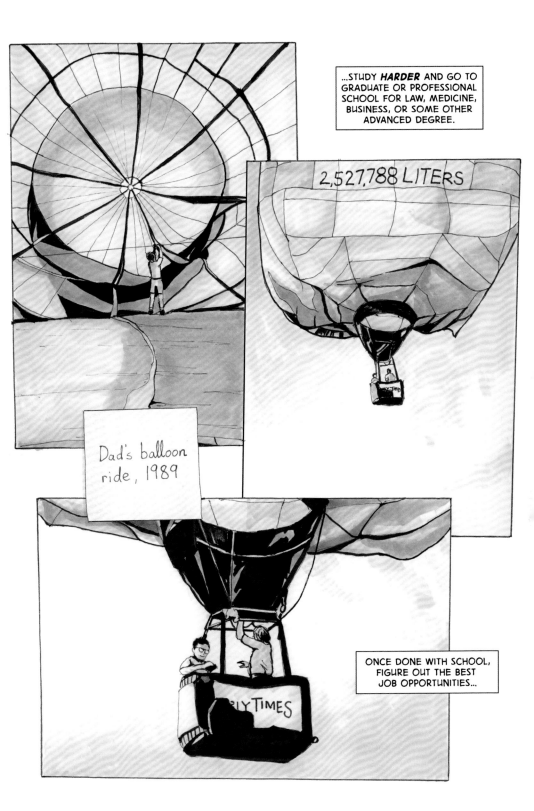

...STUDY **HARDER** AND GO TO GRADUATE OR PROFESSIONAL SCHOOL FOR LAW, MEDICINE, BUSINESS, OR SOME OTHER ADVANCED DEGREE.

2,527,788 LITERS

Dad's balloon ride, 1989

ONCE DONE WITH SCHOOL, FIGURE OUT THE BEST JOB OPPORTUNITIES...

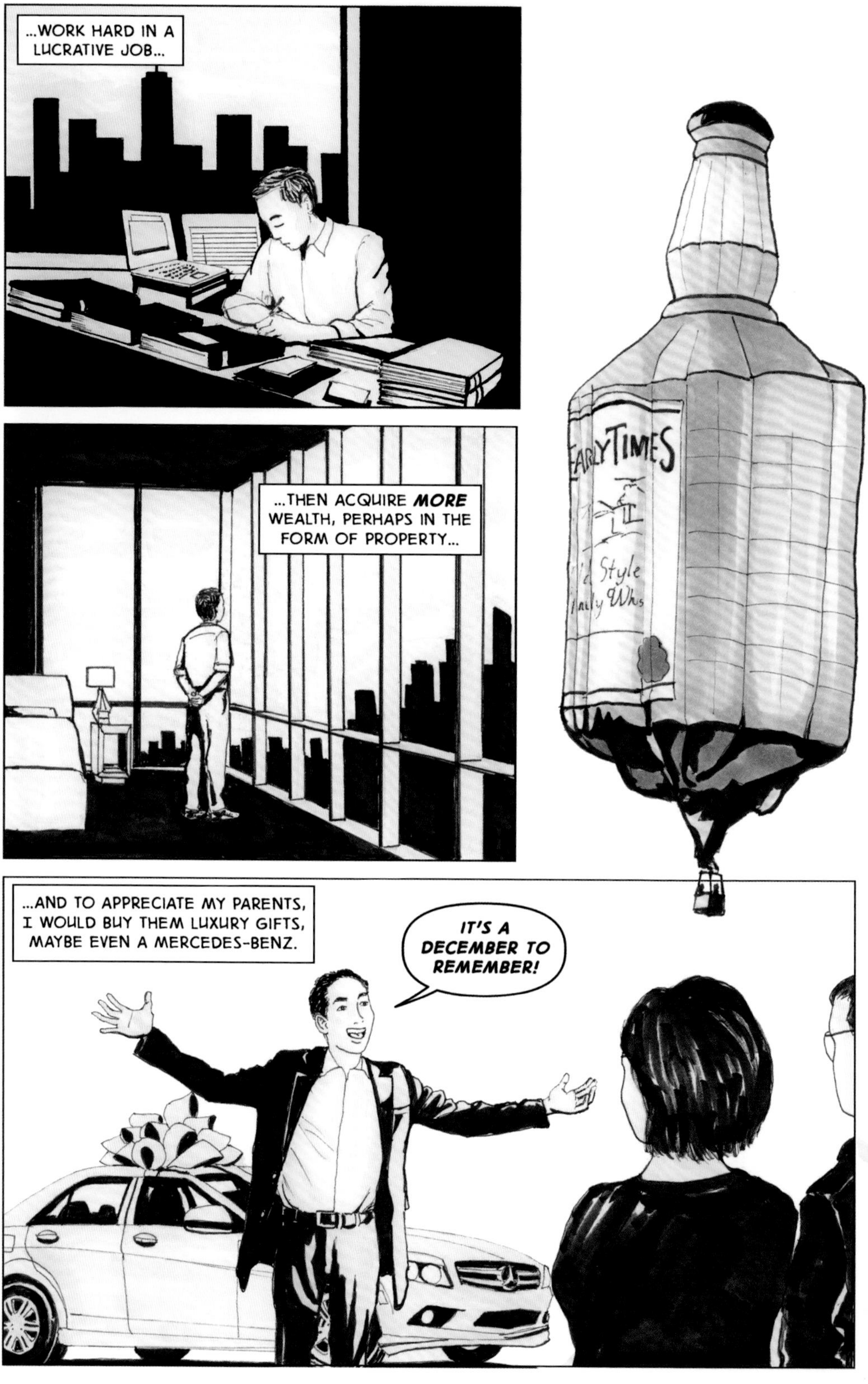
...WORK HARD IN A LUCRATIVE JOB...
...THEN ACQUIRE MORE WEALTH, PERHAPS IN THE FORM OF PROPERTY...
EARLY TIMES
...AND TO APPRECIATE MY PARENTS, I WOULD BUY THEM LUXURY GIFTS, MAYBE EVEN A MERCEDES-BENZ.
IT'S A DECEMBER TO REMEMBER!

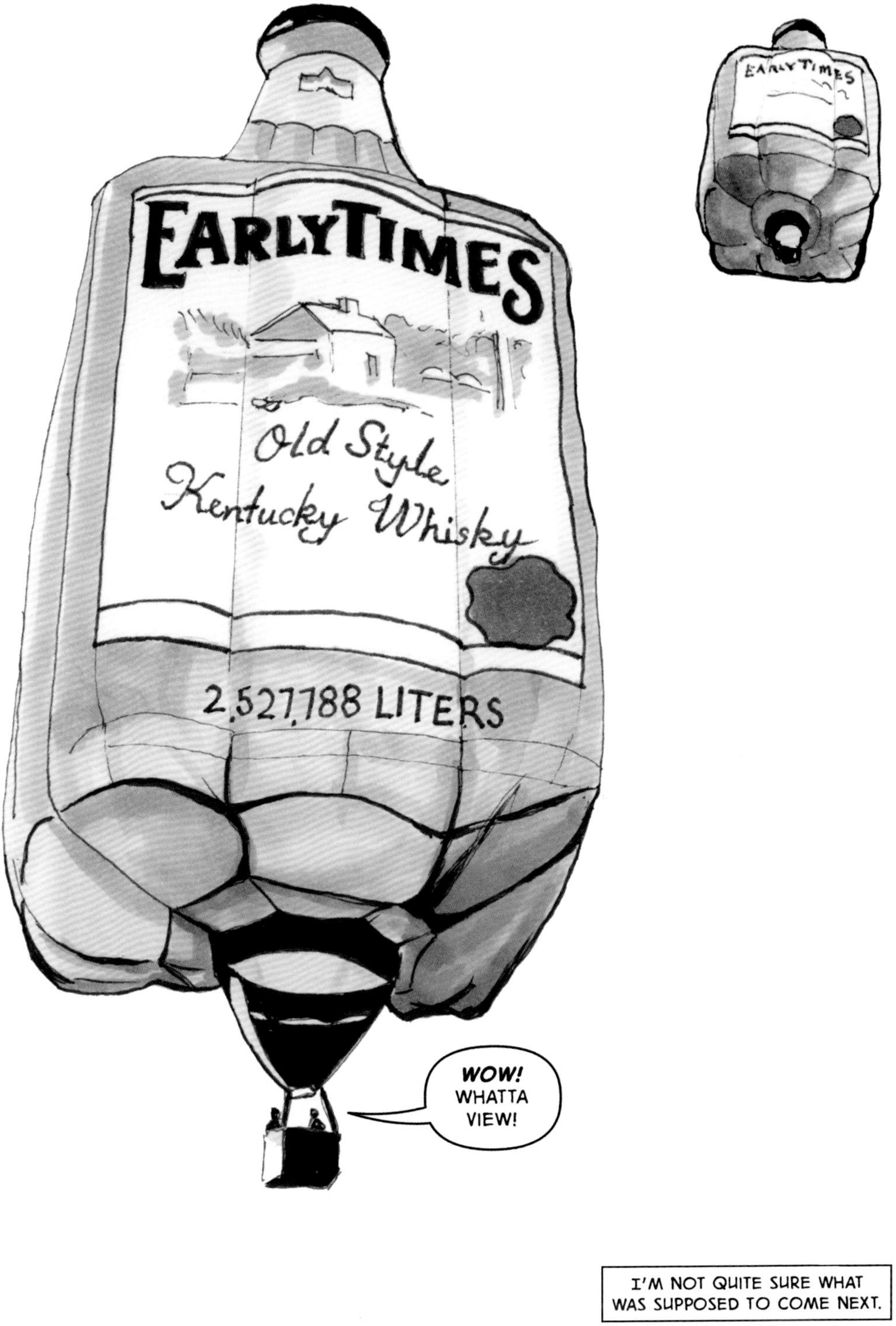

EARLY TIMES
Old Style Kentucky Whisky
2,527,788 LITERS
EARLY TIMES
WOW! WHATTA VIEW!
I'M NOT QUITE SURE WHAT WAS SUPPOSED TO COME NEXT.

ENDLESS WORK ETHIC DROVE OUR AMBITIONS OF UPWARD MOBILITY.

AND MOMENTS OF CREATIVITY BECAME A REWARD OF SORTS FOR LONG HOURS.

LONG HOURS, PUNCTUATED BY THE OCCASIONAL BREAKTHROUGH.

NOT UNLIKE THE PRACTICE OF ART.

I PASSED LOTS OF TIME DRAWING ON SCRAPS OF PAPER.

AND AS I IMAGINED WORLDS BEYOND OUR DAILY EXISTENCE IN THE STORE, MY DRAWING STEADILY IMPROVED.

I ALSO REMEMBER THE INITIAL THRILL OF TENDING REGISTER.

SMALLER TRANSACTIONS WERE ALWAYS IN CASH, AND EACH PURCHASE WOULD THEN BE WRAPPED IN A FREE PAPER BAG.

BANTER MIGHT ENSUE:

HEY, HOW ABOUT A DISCOUNT?

SURE, HOW ABOUT A *FREE BAG* DISCOUNT?

NO GRATITUDE...

...HRM. *CLEVER,* KID.

...BUT ANOTHER SMALL TRIUMPH OF CREATIVITY.

ANOTHER FAMILY TENET WAS UNFLAPPABLE CHEER AGAINST ADVERSITY.

WHEN THE FREEZER WOULD BREAK DOWN, SALES WOULD SLOW.

AND WHILE STRIKING A HOPEFUL NOTE, MY DAD WOULD APOLOGIZE TO DISAPPOINTED CUSTOMERS.

SORRY, NO COLD BEER TODAY! COME BACK MAYBE TOMORROW!

MY PATIENCE HAD ITS LIMITS THOUGH...

Oh! ooooh!!! Ahhh!!! oh! oh! oh!

...AS MY ROOMMATE BROUGHT IN ANOTHER MASSAGE THERAPIST FOR "GROUP THERAPY" SESSIONS.

GAHHH.

EVEN THOUGH MY PARENTS DIDN'T KNOW OF THIS LIVING SITUATION...

Yes!! Yesss Yes!! sss!!

I GOTTA GET OUT OF HERE.

...THIS WAS PROBABLY THE CLOSEST I GOT TO SHARING THEIR DOUBTS ABOUT MY NONPROFIT WORK.

I MOVED OUT WHILE APPLYING TO LAW SCHOOL.

THANKS FOR THE LAST TWO MONTHS.

MAYBE SEE YOU AROUND.

DESPITE NOT BEING ABLE TO SLEEP IN THE APARTMENT, I REALLY DIDN'T THINK MY ROOMMATE WAS A BAD PERSON...

...AND I EVEN GOT A FINAL SURPRISING COMMENT.

THANKS, EDDIE. YOU WERE A GREAT ROOMMATE.

OH, UH...

...THANKS.

AT THIS POINT, I HAD ACCEPTED THE LAW AS MY NEW CAREER TO FULFILL MY FAMILY'S IDEA OF SUCCESS.

BEFORE I STARTED LAW SCHOOL, MY FAMILY DID MUCH MORE THAN LIQUOR RETAIL: WHOLESALE, FINE GIFTS AND COLLECTIBLES, EXPORTS.

BUT MY STRONGEST MEMORIES ARE OF FAMILY, PATIENTLY WAITING AT THE CASH REGISTER.

WAITING FOR THE DREAM OF WHAT MY HIGHER EDUCATION COULD DO FOR THE FAMILY.

ONCE I GRADUATED FROM LAW SCHOOL WOULD I BE ABLE TO BUY A MERCEDES-BENZ AS A GIFT FOR MY PARENTS?

OR WOULD THEY HAVE THEIR MINIVAN FOREVER?

IT'S TEMPTING TO WRITE AN ENDING WHERE THE SCRAPPY UNDERDOG WINS WITH ENOUGH PERSEVERANCE.

WITH THE BEST CUSTOMER SERVICE.

AND ENOUGH FREE PAPER BAGS.

NONE OF IT WAS ENOUGH FOR CUSTOMERS TO COME BACK.

WITH DEVASTATING COMPETITION AND DWINDLING MERCHANDISE, THE STORE EVENTUALLY CLOSED.

WHEN THE YOUTH LEARNED OF MY LAW SCHOOL PLANS, THEY TRIED TO IMAGINE A SIMILAR LIFE FOR THEMSELVES.

THEY COULDN'T BELIEVE I WOULD LEAVE PLAYING FOUR SQUARE AND CREATING ART WITH THEM FOR ANYTHING ELSE.

THEY WERE JUSTIFIABLY PROUD OF THEIR WORK, BUT I NEVER PRESUMED TO TAKE CREDIT FOR THEIR SUCCESSES.

WHEN I CAME ACROSS OCCASIONALLY DARK THOUGHTS FROM THE YOUTH, I REALIZED THERE WERE ASPECTS OF THEIR LIVES I WOULD NEVER KNOW.

AS THEIR SCHOOL YEAR ENDED, I RECEIVED MORE GIFTS AND ANOTHER BATCH OF EFFUSIVE THANK-YOU NOTES.

THESE MEMENTOS REMINDED ME HOW FUN MOMENTS WITH THE YOUTH OFTEN OUTWEIGHED THE COSTS IN MY OWN LIFE.

43

I HELD ON TO THE JOYFUL MEMORIES AS MUCH AS I COULD.

YOU HAVE TO WEAR THIS ON YOUR HEAD, *OKAY??*

HAH! I'LL THINK ABOUT IT.

MY NEW SUBLET IN SF WAS TOO SMALL FOR DISPLAYING THEM, AND FOR A LONG TIME, THEY STAYED UNPACKED IN A BOX.

I STILL APPRECIATED THEIR EARNEST FINAL NOTES TO ME, SOMETIMES EVEN DISPENSING CAREER ADVICE:

Dear Eddie,
Why don't you stay and be the leader of blue group? Being a lawyer is fine, but being a leader is better!

BUT A CONVERSATION I COULD NEVER HAVE WITH THEM WAS HOW MUCH WAS ON THE LINE FOR ME.

THE SACRIFICES WERE MY BURDEN ONLY, *NOT* THEIRS. WHEN I COULD BARELY TAKE CARE OF MYSELF, LET ALONE MY FAMILY...

...I KNEW THIS CHAPTER HAD TO BE CLOSED, AND IT WAS TIME TO MOVE ON.

CHAPTER TWO

EASY MONEY

ON THE FIRST DAY OF LAW SCHOOL, WE DOVE RIGHT INTO THE MEANING OF "INTENT."

BRIAN DAILEY, *AGED 5 YEARS, 9 MONTHS*, HAD MOVED A LAWN CHAIR ON WHICH RUTH GARRATT, AN ADULT, WAS GOING TO SIT. RUTH THEN *FELL*, SUSTAINING A HIP FRACTURE AND OTHER INJURIES.

AND SHE *SUED* THE BOY!

THIS WAS MY FIRST INTRODUCTION TO PROFESSOR JOHN DIAMOND.

BESIDES *DESIRE* TO CAUSE INJURY, BRIAN CAN ALSO HAVE INTENT IF HE KNEW WITH *SUBSTANTIAL CERTAINTY* THAT RUTH WOULD SIT THERE. DOES ANYONE HERE THINK THE COURT GOT IT *WRONG?*

NO ONE IN THE CLASS SPOKE UP.

DOES ANYONE WANT TO *DENY* POOR RUTH COMPENSATION FOR HER INJURIES?

MORE CRICKETS. I REALLY WASN'T THE TYPE OF STUDENT TO SPEAK UP ON THE FIRST DAY...

...BUT I DID KNOW SOMETHING ABOUT WORKING WITH YOUTH.

THE FACTS HERE DON'T SEEM TO INDICATE INTENT. BRIAN HAD MOVED THE CHAIR A FEW FEET SIDEWAYS TO SEAT HIMSELF...

"...WHEN HE SAW THAT RUTH WAS ABOUT TO SIT DOWN, HE GOT UP IN A HURRY AND TRIED TO MOVE BACK THE CHAIR, BUT BECAUSE OF HIS 'SMALL SIZE AND LACK OF DEXTERITY,' HE COULDN'T RETURN IT IN TIME.

"BRIAN DOESN'T SEEM TO EXPECT THAT RUTH WOULD SIT DOWN IN THE SAME SPOT."

AS I ARGUED THIS, I WASN'T THINKING ABOUT THE LEGAL STANDARD SO MUCH AS THE YOUTH OF MY PRIOR WORK.

AND THIS IS HOW I FELL INTO THE PROFESSOR'S FIRST TRAP.

BUT WHAT ABOUT *SUBSTANTIAL CERTAINTY*? IF BRIAN TRULY LACKED CAPACITY TO FORM THE INTENT, WOULD HE HAVE DONE ALL THOSE ACTIONS?

I WAS STUCK HERE, BUT STILL A SKEPTIC. SUING A FIVE-YEAR-OLD SEEMED UNFAIR TO ME.

I GOT OFF EASY THAT DAY, AS PROFESSOR DIAMOND QUICKLY MOVED ON TO THE NEXT CASE IN THE TEXTBOOK.

IN THE MONTHS AHEAD, I ALSO HAD A VERY DIFFERENT EDUCATION THAT BEGAN WITH LOW-STAKES POKER GAMES WITH FRIENDS IN LAW SCHOOL.

PREVIOUSLY, I HAD DABBLED IN GAMES WITH A *$5* BUY-IN, WHICH SEEMED LIKE A LOT OF MONEY TO A NONPROFIT WORKER.

THE *$20* LAW STUDENT GAMES WERE STILL JUST SOCIAL FUN, BUT I HAD A KNACK FOR THEM.

ALRIGHT, WHAT DO WE GOT, WHAT DO WE GOT...

UGH, THIS IS *SUCH* A DUMB GAME.

IT'S *SO* SLOW.

I LIKED THE INTELLECTUAL CHALLENGE, READ A FEW BOOKS ON POKER THEORY...

...AND FOUND MYSELF QUICKLY GRADUATING TO MORE SERIOUS GAMES.

CALIFORNIA HAD DOZENS OF STATE-LICENSED CARDROOMS, WHERE I COULD GAIN MORE EXPERIENCE.

SO I BEGAN BUILDING A BANKROLL FOR NO-LIMIT TEXAS HOLD 'EM GAMES WITH A *$500* BUY-IN.

PLAYERS SOMETIMES TOOK A LONG TIME TO MAKE DECISIONS, AND THE LULLS IN THE GAME COULD BE MIND-NUMBINGLY SLOW.

FOLD.

SO TO PASS THE TIME, I TOOK TO READING.

LEGAL TEXTBOOKS WEREN'T PAGE-TURNERS, BUT THEY WERE PREP FOR MORE INTERESTING STORIES IN CLASS, IN THE FORM OF *HYPOTHETICALS*.

A HYPOTHETICAL WOULD VARY THE FACTS OF A CASE TO TEST UNDERSTANDING OF THE LAW.

FOR INSTANCE, IS IT AN ASSAULT IN TORTS IF SOMEONE THROWS A ROCK OR PIE AT SANDY *WHILE SHE'S NOT LOOKING?*

INVARIABLY, STUDENTS WOULD NOD ALONG, AND PROFESSOR DIAMOND WOULD POUNCE.

IF YOU THOUGHT "YES," YOU'D BE **TRAPPED!**

NO! THEY HAVE TO BE AWARE PRIOR TO THE ATTACK.

EXCITED TO EXPLAIN THE LAW, PROFESSOR DIAMOND WOULD GLEEFULLY PUMP HIS ARMS BACK AND FORTH...

...A TYPE OF PHYSICALITY THAT WAS ABSENT AT THE POKER TABLE.

SHIFTING YOUR BODY CREATED *TELLS*, SIGNALS THAT COULD GIVE AWAY YOUR HAND. SO I ADOPTED UNCOMFORTABLE POSTURES WITH LITTLE MOVEMENT.

POKER'S ECONOMY OF MOVEMENT ALSO KEPT ME FOCUSED.

EACH GAME HAD ITS OWN DYNAMICS AND PLAYERS...

...AND AS WITH THE LAW, A RESPONSE COULD CHANGE BASED ON VARIATIONS IN ENVIRONMENT AND FACT.

LET'S SAY GERTRUDE CONFINES A STRANGER, SAMMY, IN A ROOM...

...IS IT *FALSE IMPRISONMENT* OF SAMMY IF GERTRUDE ASKS HER LOYAL HITMAN TO GO OVER *IN 15 MINUTES* TO "TAKE CARE OF" SAMMY IF HE LEAVES?

WHAT! I'M EATING HERE, TRUDY!

IF YOU SAID "YES," YOU'D BE

TRAPPED!

NO, THERE'S NO *IMMEDIATE* THREAT.

SO SAMMY CAN'T CLAIM FALSE IMPRISONMENT.

THE APPLICATION OF LAW WAS OFTEN *COUNTERINTUITIVE* TO A LAYPERSON...

...AND PROFESSOR DIAMOND PLAYED AGAINST THOSE EXPECTATIONS TO SET HIS TRAPS.

RAISE... 50 TO GO.

I APPLIED THIS LESSON TO POKER BY CHANGING UP MY BETTING PATTERNS AND RANGE OF HANDS IN A GAME.

HIT THE FLUSH ON THE FLOP.

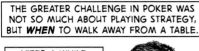

THE GREATER CHALLENGE IN POKER WAS NOT SO MUCH ABOUT PLAYING STRATEGY, BUT **WHEN** TO WALK AWAY FROM A TABLE.

AFTER A WHILE, CHIPS BECAME LESS ABOUT THE MONEY, AND MORE ABOUT KEEPING SCORE.

WHY STOP AT TWO RACKS OF CHIPS, WHEN YOU COULD WIN **FOUR?**

WHY STOP AT FOUR RACKS, WHEN YOU COULD WIN **EIGHT?**

OF COURSE, REALITY OFTEN THREW COLD WATER ON FANTASIES OF RUNNING UP THE SCORE.

UNLIKE GAMES WITH CAPPED BETTING, YOU COULD LOSE **ALL** YOUR CHIPS IN A SINGLE HAND OF NO-LIMIT HOLD 'EM.

WHENEVER I SAT DOWN FOR A NEW GAME, I WAS SOMEWHAT PREPARED TO GO THROUGH THESE WILD SWINGS.

BUT EVEN WITH MY CAREFUL PREP TO MINIMIZE LOSSES AGAINST LOOSE PLAYERS AND DEEPER CHIP STACKS...

...IT WAS EASY TO FALL INTO THE TRAP OF OVERCONFIDENCE.

51

ALL IN.

I COULD BET WITH A STRONG STARTING HAND AND STILL SEE IT ALL SLIP AWAY...

...CALL.

WITH THE TURN OF ANOTHER CARD.

ONCE A HAND WAS DONE AND SHOWN, OTHER PLAYERS WOULD WEIGH IN.

BAD BEAT THERE.

OUCH, HE CAUGHT THAT ACE ON THE RIVER.

AT LEAST YOU DID WHAT YOU COULD TO PROTECT YOUR QUEENS.

BUT SYMPATHETIC WORDS DIDN'T MEAN MUCH.

THERE WAS NO RETURN ON BAD LUCK OR LOUSY DECISIONS. JUST MONEY *LOST.*

REBUYING INTO A GAME SOMETIMES MADE SENSE, BUT NOT IF IT WAS DRIVEN BY AN EMOTIONAL NEED TO WIN BACK MONEY.

REBUY?

NO, THANKS. *DONE.*

SINCE I WAS ALREADY USED TO THE THRIFTY EATING HABITS OF A STUDENT, I WAS ABLE TO CUT MYSELF OFF FROM POKER BEFORE GOING ON TILT.

A CAN OF BEANS OR SOUP WOULD TIDE ME OVER UNTIL THE NEXT LOAN DISBURSEMENT.

I HAD HEARD LAW PROFESSORS WARN ABOUT **GOLDEN HANDCUFFS,** WHICH WENT LIKE THIS:

A NEW LAWYER STARTS WITH A LARGE FIRM SALARY, AND THEN ADOPTS A HIGH COST OF LIVING, LIKE PRICEY DINNERS, CARS, AND HOUSES...

...AND TO SUSTAIN THIS LIFESTYLE, BECOMES *TRAPPED* IN THE JOB.

ON THE OTHER HAND, MY MOTHER HAD A ROSIER VIEW ABOUT THE LIVES OF OTHER LAW SCHOOL GRADUATES.

...SO ONCE HE GRADUATED, HE GOT A MERCEDES S-CLASS FOR HIS PARENTS.

MM-HMM.

I KNEW MY PARENTS DIDN'T CARE ABOUT THE DOLLAR VALUE OF THIS CAR.

GIFTS WERE REALLY ABOUT THE ACT OF GENEROSITY AND RESPECT.

AND BECAUSE OF THE GOOD RETURNS IN POKER, I KEPT COMING BACK TO THE GAME.

WITH READY ACCESS TO CASH, I COULD PAY FOR DRINKS OR DINNER FOR OTHERS.

I ENJOYED MAKING THESE GESTURES ESPECIALLY SINCE MY LAW SCHOOL FRIENDS AND I WERE PREOCCUPIED WITH CHEAP EATS AND STUDENT DEBT...

...LEADING TO THE INEVITABLE QUESTION AND ANSWER:

SO...WHAT KINDA LAW DO YOU WANT TO PRACTICE?

THE *MONEY-MAKING* KIND.

THE TRUTH WAS THAT I HAD NO IDEA HOW TO PURSUE BOTH COMMUNITY WORK AND EASY MONEY AS A LAWYER.

MY IDEAS OF A LEGAL CAREER WERE INSPIRED BY JOHN GRISHAM NOVELS AND A PHOTOBOOTH I ONCE FOUND IN A BAR.

Services
Divorce
Gambling
Defamation
Small Claims
Personal Injury
Penal Offenses
Paternity Tests
Traffic Violations

Photos
Delivere
Digitall
5
Pay with
credit

WITH SO MUCH READING ON A DAILY BASIS, LAW SCHOOL ITSELF DIDN'T PROVIDE MUCH TIME TO EXPLORE DIFFERENT CAREERS.

THE CASE LAW BEING POURED INTO MY HEAD WAS DENSE AND DRY...

...SO CLASS DISCUSSIONS INFLUENCED MY CAREER CHOICES MUCH MORE THAN TEXTBOOKS.

...SOUND REASONABLE, EDDIE?

...SURE.

WELL...

...ANOTHER *NOTCH* ON MY BELT!

hehe haha
HEHE
HAHAHA hehe
HAHAHA

ALL KIDDING ASIDE, PROFESSOR DIAMOND DID SPARK MY INITIAL INTEREST IN *CIVIL LITIGATION*...

PART-TIME WORK AT LAW FIRMS HELPED ME BETTER UNDERSTAND LEGAL MOTIONS AND CASELOADS.

♪

BZzzzz

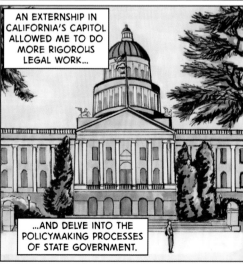

AN EXTERNSHIP IN CALIFORNIA'S CAPITOL ALLOWED ME TO DO MORE RIGOROUS LEGAL WORK...

...AND DELVE INTO THE POLICYMAKING PROCESSES OF STATE GOVERNMENT.

LEARNING HOW LAWS WERE PASSED AND IMPLEMENTED MADE ME APPRECIATE LEGAL AND POLICY ADVOCACY AS TWO SIDES OF THE SAME COIN.

LEGISLATIVE OFFICE BUILDING

STATIONED AT MY CUBBYHOLE DESK, I GOT TO EXPLORE ENVIRONMENTAL AND SOCIAL JUSTICE ISSUES WITH OTHER ATTORNEYS OF THE ASSEMBLY JUDICIARY COMMITTEE.

THE LEGISLATIVE PROCESS TOOK INPUT FROM DIFFERENT PERSPECTIVES, INCLUDING PRIVATE SECTOR COMPANIES, NONPROFITS, OTHER GOVERNMENT AGENCIES, AND MORE.

WHILE CONTINUING THESE STUDIES, I KEPT COMING BACK TO THE MORE INSULAR WORLD OF LOCAL CARD CLUBS.

THE CONVERSATIONS OFTEN FOCUSED ON POKER ITSELF...

...SUCH AS WITH THE DEALERS.

SO DO YOU EVER PLAY?

NO.

EVEN IN THIS CURT ANSWER, ONE COULD SENSE A WORLD-WEARY RECOGNITION OF THE DOWNSIDES OF GAMBLING...

...BUT POINTING TO ME, SHE ALSO ADDED:

IF I PLAYED LIKE *HIM*, I WOULD.

WHAT, *ME?*

NO.

THE DEALER MEANT THIS AS A COMPLIMENT, BUT I FELT SELF-CONSCIOUS ABOUT PLAYING WAY TOO MUCH...

...WHICH ALSO MADE ME THINK THAT POKER WAS CAUSING NEW PROBLEMS.

SINCE I WAS ALWAYS RUSHING BETWEEN POKER, CLASSES, AND LEGAL JOBS, I HAD FORGOTTEN TO EAT LUNCH AGAIN--SO I DISMISSED THE INITIAL FEELING OF LIGHTHEADEDNESS AS HUNGER.

BUT THEN, IT WAS LIKE A CURTAIN DROPPING OVER THE RIGHT EYE.

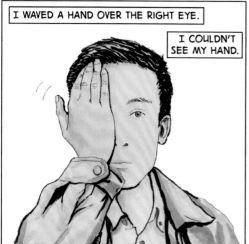

I WAVED A HAND OVER THE RIGHT EYE.

I COULDN'T SEE MY HAND.

CONFUSED, I STRAINED TO SEE OUT OF THE RIGHT EYE BY COVERING THE LEFT...

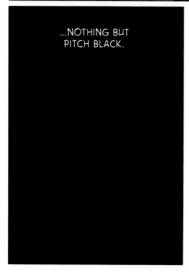

...NOTHING BUT PITCH BLACK.

THE BLINDNESS PASSED AFTER A FEW SECONDS.

AND THE INCIDENT ELICITED A SINGLE THOUGHT:

wtf.

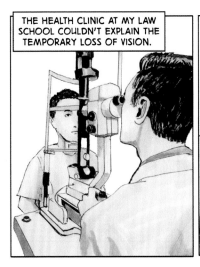

THE HEALTH CLINIC AT MY LAW SCHOOL COULDN'T EXPLAIN THE TEMPORARY LOSS OF VISION.

AS THE PERIODS OF BLINDNESS INCREASED IN FREQUENCY, I WAS REFERRED TO SPECIALISTS, WHO PRESCRIBED MORE TESTS.

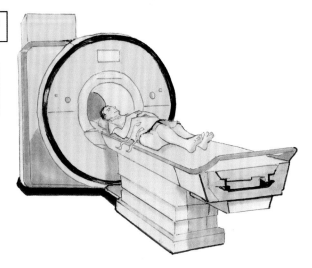

SPECULATION ON CAUSES RANGED FROM A BRAIN TUMOR TO MULTIPLE SCLEROSIS.

OPHTHALMOLOGISTS, NEUROLOGISTS, AND NEURO-OPHTHALMOLOGISTS ALL PUZZLED OVER MY PARTIAL BLINDNESS, AND THEY ORDERED MORE TESTS.

MORE BLOODWORK, X-RAYS, MRI AND CT SCANS.

MORE WAITING.

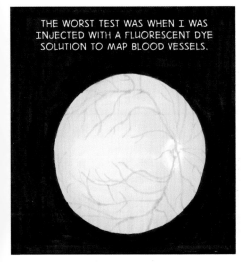

THE WORST TEST WAS WHEN I WAS INJECTED WITH A FLUORESCENT DYE SOLUTION TO MAP BLOOD VESSELS.

THE SOLUTION INDUCED NAUSEA, AND I ENDED UP DRY HEAVING INTO A BASKET.

hurk!

STILL, NO EXPLANATION.

MOST TESTS WEREN'T TOO BAD...JUST MONOTONOUS AND TIME-CONSUMING.

WHILE IN WAITING ROOMS, I WOULD TRY TO CATCH UP ON READING.

SCHOOL ROUTINES WERE COMFORTING.

BUT THE VISION LOSS DISRUPTED ROUTINE, INCLUDING ACTIVITIES LIKE MOOT COURT.

THIS COURT SHOULD REVERSE THE LOWER COURT FOR THE FOLLOWING TWO REASONS:

FIRST, CONSTANT MONITORING BY THE GOVERNMENT EVISCERATES MR. HAN'S RIGHT TO EFFECTIVE COUNSEL...

...BY IMPEDING THE FREE EXCHANGE OF INFORMATION BETWEEN ATTORNEY AND CLIENT.

WHILE I STUMBLED THROUGH ORAL ARGUMENT, I DIDN'T WANT TO BURDEN ANYONE WITH WHAT HAD JUST HAPPENED.

I COULDN'T EVEN BRING MYSELF TO CALL MY PARENTS.

THE GREAT RECESSION WAS UNDERWAY IN LATE 2008, AND THE FAMILY BUSINESS WAS DOING POORLY.

IT WAS A TERRIBLE TIME TO STRESS OUT MY PARENTS WITH THE UNEXPLAINABLE.

I DIDN'T CALL THEM EVEN WHEN A SHALLOW RETINAL DETACHMENT WAS FOUND AND REQUIRED A SCLERAL BUCKLE.

THE FOLLOWING WEEKS WERE A BLUR AS I SHIFTED CLASSWORK AROUND THE NEEDED SURGERY.

IT WAS *PROFESSOR DIAMOND* WHO SLOWED ME DOWN.

UNIVERSITY OF CALIFORNIA
HASTINGS COLLEGE OF THE LAW

WELL, EDDIE...

...IT SOUNDS LIKE YOU'RE PLANNING FOR EVERYTHING.

AND IT'S ALWAYS *GOOD* TO PLAN, BUT PLEASE CONSIDER SOMETHING ELSE.

I UNDERSTAND YOUR PARENTS HAVE THE BUSINESS, BUT THEY ARE YOUR FAMILY.

I KNOW IF IT WERE MY SON, I WOULD VERY MUCH WANT TO KNOW.

YOUR PARENTS, THEY WOULD VERY MUCH WANT TO KNOW.

...*OK.* THANKS, PROFESSOR.

IN 2017, I TOOK TIME OFF WORK TO SUPPORT MY MOTHER AS SHE UNDERWENT TESTING IN SEOUL.

세브란스병원 SEVERANCE HOSPITAL

THE TRIP REMINDED ME OF THE 2008 SURGERY WHEN SHE DROPPED EVERYTHING TO TAKE CARE OF ME.

SHE SUFFERED FROM FAINTING SPELLS SINCE 2005, AND TESTS IN THE U.S. HAD FAILED TO FIND ANYTHING.

외래·병동입구

EVEN AS SHE WENT INTO THE HOSPITAL, SHE WORRIED ABOUT MY WORKLOAD BACK HOME.

ARE YOU SURE YOU CAN TAKE TIME OFF, EDDIE?

NOVEMBER 4, 2008

SO...

...DID YOU VOTE YET?

YEP, JUST DID THIS MORNING.

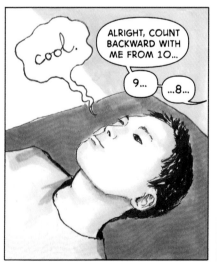

cool.

ALRIGHT, COUNT BACKWARD WITH ME FROM 10...

9...

...8...

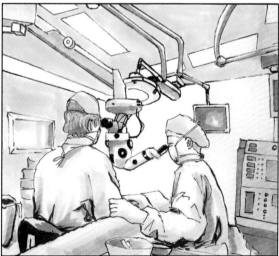

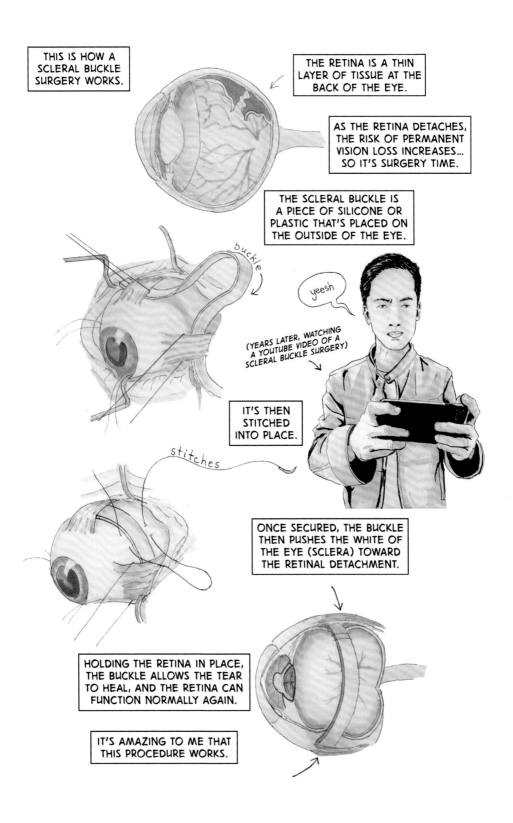

THIS IS HOW A SCLERAL BUCKLE SURGERY WORKS.

THE RETINA IS A THIN LAYER OF TISSUE AT THE BACK OF THE EYE.

AS THE RETINA DETACHES, THE RISK OF PERMANENT VISION LOSS INCREASES... SO IT'S SURGERY TIME.

THE SCLERAL BUCKLE IS A PIECE OF SILICONE OR PLASTIC THAT'S PLACED ON THE OUTSIDE OF THE EYE.

buckle

yeesh

(YEARS LATER, WATCHING A YOUTUBE VIDEO OF A SCLERAL BUCKLE SURGERY)

IT'S THEN STITCHED INTO PLACE.

stitches

ONCE SECURED, THE BUCKLE THEN PUSHES THE WHITE OF THE EYE (SCLERA) TOWARD THE RETINAL DETACHMENT.

HOLDING THE RETINA IN PLACE, THE BUCKLE ALLOWS THE TEAR TO HEAL, AND THE RETINA CAN FUNCTION NORMALLY AGAIN.

IT'S AMAZING TO ME THAT THIS PROCEDURE WORKS.

NOT EVERYTHING IN HOSPITALS WORKED WELL, HOWEVER...

I'LL GO GET SNACKS AND DRINKS, *UMMA.* ANYTHING ELSE?

HOW ABOUT THE *WI-FI* PASSWORD?

I COULDN'T LOG ON...DON'T SEE A TV REMOTE EITHER.

US AIMS TO INCREASE PRESSURE

IT WOULD BE NICE FOR YOU TO WATCH SOMETHING ELSE...

...ANYTHING ELSE BESIDES THE NEWS.

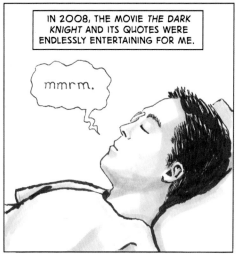

IN 2008, THE MOVIE *THE DARK KNIGHT* AND ITS QUOTES WERE ENDLESSLY ENTERTAINING FOR ME.

mmrm.

HOW ARE YOU FEELING, EDDIE?

"REMEMBER THAT NAME YOU HAD FOR ME WHEN I WAS AT INTERNAL AFFAIRS?"

"WHAT WAS IT, *GORDON?*

"SAY IT."

...YOUR MOM IS GETTING THE CAR.

ONCE YOU'RE READY, I'LL HELP YOU TO THE GARAGE.

AWW.

NO SENSE OF HUMOR, THIS GUY.

OUR FAMILY USUALLY FOUND HUMOR EVEN IN TERRIBLE TIMES.

ACTIONS LIKE COOKING AND FOOD DELIVERY SHOWED OUR CARE FOR EACH OTHER.

GOT TREATS FOR LATER.

MMM.

HEY, *LOOK,* MA...

BUT HUMOR WAS MORE EFFECTIVE FOR COPING.

HUMOR COULD CHANGE OUR STATE OF MIND ABOUT TRAGEDY...

...I'M ON TV.

...WHETHER FOR MYSELF...

I'LL TAKE A PICTURE FOR THE REST OF THE FAMILY.

...OR FOR THE COMMUNITY.

RIGHT AFTER MY OWN EYE SURGERY IN 2008, WE WATCHED THE NEWS.

≈bzzz bzzz≈

HEY. YEAH, WATCHING IT NOW.

PRETTY COOL.

ALTHOUGH DRUGGED OUT OF MY MIND ON PAINKILLERS, I STILL APPRECIATED THE NIGHT AS HISTORIC.

AMA ELECTED PRESIDENT [LIVE]

2017 WAS ALSO EVENTFUL.

TRUMP WILL LIKELY NOT VISIT DMZ

HE SAYS ANYTHING, DOESN'T HE?

IT WAS THE SAME YEAR THAT TRUMP PROMISED NORTH KOREA WOULD SEE *"FIRE AND FURY LIKE THE WORLD HAS NEVER SEEN,"* RISKING ANOTHER KOREAN WAR.

WHAT KIND OF LEADER IS THIS?

IN SOME MOMENTS, IT WAS HARDER TO FIND A PUNCH LINE.

WHEN THE FIRST ROUND OF BANDAGES CAME OFF, I INSPECTED MY EYE UNDER THE PLEASANT HAZE OF PAINKILLERS.

HRMM.

AT A DISTANCE, EVERYTHING SEEMED FINE.

UPON CLOSER INSPECTION, MY ENTIRE EYE SEEMED TO BE FILLED WITH BLOOD.

IT WOULD TAKE MONTHS FOR THIS EYE TO ADJUST AND HEAL PROPERLY.

I REALIZED I NEEDED TO RELY ON MY OTHER EYE FOR EVERYTHING.

GAHH, I LOOK LIKE A JAMES BOND VILLAIN.

DESPITE SOME GENTLE SUGGESTIONS TO DELAY MY EXAMS AND ADD ONE MORE SEMESTER OF LAW SCHOOL, I WAS UNWILLING TO TAKE ON MORE LAW SCHOOL DEBT.

WORKING MOSTLY FROM BED, I PLOWED AHEAD TO KEEP MY GRADUATION ON TRACK.

TO AVOID MORE EYE STRAIN, I FOCUSED ON LAW SCHOOL READING OVER DRAWING...

AND I WORRIED ABOUT MY HEALTH PERMANENTLY STOPPING MY CREATIVITY.

THERE WERE SOME PERMANENT EFFECTS AFTER THE SURGERY.

THE SCLERAL BUCKLE RESHAPED MY RIGHT EYE, SIGNIFICANTLY WORSENING MY MYOPIA.

MOREOVER, THE RETINAL DETACHMENT HAD LED TO A PERMANENT LOSS OF PERIPHERAL VISION.

HELLO, EDDIE!

I COULDN'T SEE MUCH OF THE WORLD TO MY RIGHT SIDE.

OCCASIONALLY AT WORK EVENTS, IT TAKES ME SOME EXTRA TIME TO RECOGNIZE PEOPLE.

I USUALLY DON'T BOTHER EXPLAINING WHY.

HELLO, EDDIE!

STILL, THE DOCTORS WERE SATISFIED THE SCLERAL BUCKLE HAD FIXED THE BOUTS OF BLINDNESS.

GENERALLY, A HAPPY RESULT.

IT'S NOT LIKE I NEED PERIPHERAL VISION TO SURVIVE IN A JUNGLE ENVIRONMENT.

ALL THINGS CONSIDERED, LIFE TURNED OUT OK.

WHILE UNEXPLAINED, FAINTING SPELLS RARELY AFFECT MY MOM NOW.

I CAN STILL DRAW AND READ THE LAW.

HEY.

HEY, MY MAN.

KEEP YOUR RIGHT UP.

AND IF I'VE LEARNED ANYTHING...

...GOOD-HUMORED RESOLVE HAS TURNED OUT TO BE A DECENT RESPONSE TO MOST TROUBLES.

AFTER ALL, IF YOU CAN'T FIND HUMOR IN YOUR OWN TRAGEDY...

YOU SHOULD SEE THE OTHER GUY.

Heh heh heh Heh heh heh

...THEN WHO WILL?

WHEN I FINALLY HEALED, I RETURNED TO POKER. TO MAKE SURE MY TIME WAS EFFICIENTLY SPENT, I BEGAN RECORDING HOURS SPENT AS WELL AS PROFIT AND LOSSES FROM EACH POKER SESSION.

STILL, I WASN'T ENJOYING MYSELF ANYMORE.

HANDS WERE STARTING TO FEEL REPETITIVE TO ME...

...EVEN IF THEY COULD BE PLAYED DIFFERENTLY.

OOF, ACE AGAIN ON THE RIVER. *FOLD.*

IN LOCAL CARDROOMS, I DIDN'T ENJOY SOCIALIZING MUCH EITHER.

I REMEMBER ONE SURLY PLAYER, WHO BET WITH SUCH EXCRUTIATING SLOWNESS...

...THAT TIME ITSELF SEEMED TO PROTECT HIS SMALL, DWINDLING CHIP STACK.

I TOOK A FEW MINUTES TO GO TO THE RESTROOM...

...BUT WHEN I RETURNED, EVERYONE HAD LEFT THE TABLE EXCEPT FOR A CARDROOM STAFFER TRYING TO SCRUB *STAINS* OUT OF THE FELT.

I WAS TOLD THERE HAD BEEN A **FREAK ACCIDENT** AS A CARD WAS DEALT TO THE SURLY PLAYER: THE EDGE OF THE CARD HAD CUT HIS HAND'S THIN SKIN...

...SPRAYING SMALL STREAKS OF BLOOD ACROSS THE TABLE.

TO WHICH I SAID:

UHM, THAT'S SOMETHING THAT CAN HAPPEN?

FROM MY FAMILY, I KNEW THAT GAMES COULD BE ISOLATING.

ACCORDING TO MY MOM, MY GRANDFATHER WAS VERY SKILLED IN PLAYING **GO**.

FAMILY MEMBERS WERE EAGER FOR AN OPPORTUNITY TO PLAY AND LEARN FROM HIM, BUT HE RARELY WAS IN A GOOD MOOD TO PLAY.

OCCASIONALLY, HE PLAYED IN LOCAL TOURNAMENTS, WHERE HIS FEES WOULD BE WAIVED AND PEOPLE WOULD GATHER TO WATCH HIM PLAY.

BUT MOSTLY, HE SPENT HOURS ALONE STUDYING GO PUZZLES.

FROM WATCHING HIM WHILE GROWING UP, MY MOM THOUGHT GO WAS A GAME LIKE SOLITAIRE, INSTEAD OF INVOLVING TWO PLAYERS.

AS I SAW UNHEALTHY CONSEQUENCES IN MY OWN GAME...

...I NEVER FELT MORE **ALONE,** EVEN WHEN SURROUNDED BY PEOPLE.

I CASHED OUT MY LAST GAME WITH LITTLE FANFARE...

LEAVING QUICK, *EH?*

YEP, NOT UP BY MUCH, BUT *OH WELL.*

NO, THAT'S *GOOD.* LEAVE EARLY WHILE YOU CAN.

...AND I WAS REASSURED ABOUT MY ESCAPE BY THE CASHIER'S COMMENT.

THERE WAS *NEVER* ANY FINALITY TO THIS LIFESTYLE, AND EVEN IF THERE WAS ONE MORE HAND THAT WON IT ALL...

...I STILL WOULD HAVE FELT TRAPPED.

WHEN I GRADUATED IN 2009, THE GREAT RECESSION HAD GUTTED THE JOB MARKET. IN RESPONSE, MY LAW SCHOOL AWARDED SMALL GRANTS TO PURSUE PUBLIC INTEREST WORK, AND I RECEIVED ONE.

NOT MUCH, BUT IT'LL DO FOR A BIT.

MY FAMILY ACCEPTED THIS CAREER CHOICE AS MAKING TEMPORARY SENSE BASED ON THE BAD ECONOMY, AND I SOUGHT SOMETHING RELATED TO MY PAST ENVIRONMENTAL AND SOCIAL JUSTICE WORK AS A LAW EXTERN.

THE MOST NATURAL FIT WAS A SMALL NONPROFIT IN SAN FRANCISCO WORKING ON LOCAL ENVIRONMENTAL JUSTICE ISSUES.

THIS NONDESCRIPT OFFICE WOULD BECOME THE BIGGEST GAMBLE OF MY LIFE.

AS FOR MY POKER WINNINGS, I NEVER GOT TO SPLURGE ON A TRIP TO PARADISE.

WHILE BASKING IN MY MODEST ACCOMPLISHMENT STORED IN AN OLD CANDY BOX, I KNEW THERE WOULD BE LEAN YEARS AHEAD.

THIS BOX BECAME THE FIX FOR MANY NEEDS, FROM GROCERIES TO UTILITIES TO RENT.

IN THE END, THE ONLY THING *EASY* ABOUT THIS HARD-WON MONEY WAS *SPENDING IT.*

BUT FORTUNATELY, ONCE THE BOX WAS EMPTY, I NEVER WANTED TO GO BACK TO THE GAME.

I HAD LEARNED HOW QUICKLY MONEY COULD COME AND GO...

...AND MOST IMPORTANTLY, I KNEW *ENOUGH* TO NOT FALL INTO THE SAME OLD TRAP.

CHAPTER THREE

IMPERFECT
SIGNALS

MY WORK AS A NONPROFIT ATTORNEY BEGAN WITH WATCHING REGULATORY HEARINGS.

YOUR HONOR, THE PROPOSED INCREASE IS *VERY* REASONABLE...

IN ONE HEARING, A PRESENTATION ARGUED FOR BILL INCREASES THAT UTILITY COMPANIES COULD CHARGE THEIR CUSTOMERS.

...IT'S *ONLY* $4 DOLLARS A MONTH...

THE PRESENTER'S SMUG TONE MADE ME UNEASY.

...LESS THAN A CUP OF COFFEE!

HIS ANALOGY WOULDN'T MAKE MUCH SENSE TO LOW-INCOME HOUSEHOLDS STRUGGLING TO GET BY...

...ESPECIALLY SINCE THEIR BILLS WEREN'T MEASURED BY CUPS OF EXPENSIVE TAKEOUT COFFEE.

ALTHOUGH LEGAL MOTIONS WERE EVEN *LESS* RELATABLE, THESE FILINGS SHAPED ENVIRONMENTAL POLICIES AND THEIR ECONOMIC IMPACTS.

Rules of Practice and Procedure

BENEFITS RANGED FROM LOWERING UTILITY BILLS TO CREATING INCENTIVES FOR RENEWABLE ENERGY AND ENERGY EFFICIENCY.

SO I SPENT A LOT OF TIME DRAFTING LEGAL AND POLICY ARGUMENTS...

IN THESE EARLY DAYS, THERE WERE PASSIVE-AGGRESSIVE REACTIONS FROM INSTITUTIONAL INTERESTS WHO DID NOT BELIEVE IN RENEWABLE ENERGY.

YES, I DID READ YOUR PIECE ON SOLAR...

...IT WAS... *CREATIVE.*

IN OTHER INSTANCES, REACTIONS WERE MORE PERSONAL.

YOU'RE SO *YOUNG...* YOU WOULDN'T UNDERSTAND.

AND I REMEMBER THIS BEING REPEATED FOR EMPHASIS...

YOU'RE *SO* YOUNG.

...AS IF ONE'S YOUTH SHOULD *AUTOMATICALLY* DISCREDIT IDEAS FOR CHANGE AND DELEGITIMIZE ACTIVISM.

STILL, IT WAS IMPORTANT NOT TO DWELL ON ANY PERSON'S NEGATIVITY.

SKILLED ADVOCATES WORKED AROUND OPPOSITION AND COULD TOGGLE BACK AND FORTH BETWEEN LOCAL, STATE, AND FEDERAL GOVERNMENT AGENCIES.

MY NONPROFIT WORK FREQUENTLY INVOLVED TRACKING STATE POLICIES IN ENVIRONMENTAL PROTECTION AND CLEAN ENERGY--AND A CAR BECAME ESSENTIAL FOR QUICK TRIPS BETWEEN THE BAY AREA AND GOVERNMENT AGENCIES IN SACRAMENTO.

MY CAR, A 2009 TOYOTA COROLLA, WASN'T THAT SPECIAL, BUT I TOOK PRIDE IN ITS FUNCTIONALITY AND LOW-MAINTENANCE NEEDS.

1hr 22min
87.9 miles

Sacramento

San Francisco

PLUS, I ENJOYED HAVING A CD PLAYER TO LISTEN TO OLD SONGS DURING THE LONG DRIVES.

ALL THE LEAVES ARE BROWN...AND THE SKY IS GRAY...

MY CAR ALSO ALLOWED ME TO TRAVEL TO A GOVERNMENT HEARING WHERE I MET AN SF COMMUNITY LEADER, ESPANOLA JACKSON.

WATCHING HER SPEAK, I LEARNED HOW HER WORDS AND AUTHENTICITY HIGHLIGHTED ENVIRONMENTAL INJUSTICES.

I BEGAN TO DEVELOP MY OWN STYLE AND EVOLVE RAPIDLY AS A PUBLIC SPEAKER.

BUT BY 2013, ISSUES AROSE FROM DRIVING MY CAR IN SF.

HEY!

IT TOOK ME A MOMENT TO REALIZE WHAT WAS GOING ON.

HEY, WE'RE OVER HERE--

AS I TURNED WITHOUT PULLING OVER, I SAW THEIR AWKWARD REALIZATION IN FLAGGING A TOTAL STRANGER.

OH.

IN THE EARLY YEARS OF RIDESHARING, MANY UBER CARS DIDN'T HAVE SIGNAGE, SO RIDES WERE OFTEN IDENTIFIED BY MAKE/MODEL.

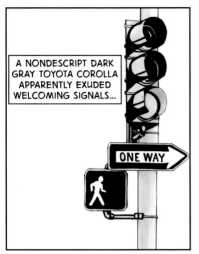

A NONDESCRIPT DARK GRAY TOYOTA COROLLA APPARENTLY EXUDED WELCOMING SIGNALS...

ONE WAY

...ESPECIALLY WHEN I WAS STATIONARY.

ONCE NEAR DIVISADERO, WHILE I WAS PARKED AND CHECKING MY PHONE...

...A STRANGER CONFIDENTLY TRIED TO OPEN THE BACK DOOR TO MY CAR.

THE LOCKED DOOR HANDLE CLICKED USELESSLY AS IT WAS REPEATEDLY PULLED.

ON A LEVEL, THIS WAS AMUSING. IT DIDN'T BOTHER ME THAT MUCH TO BE MISTAKEN FOR A RIDE.

BUT THE PRESUMPTUOUSNESS WAS PALPABLE, SOMETHING I KNEW FROM WORKING IN FOOD SERVICE AND AS A CASHIER.

THERE WASN'T ANY DIALOGUE BETWEEN US.

JUST A BLANK STARE AND SLOW REALIZATION THAT THIS WASN'T THE CAR.

THE STRANGER WALKED ON, STILL ENGROSSED IN ANOTHER CONVERSATION AND AS IF NOTHING HAD HAPPENED.

ANOTHER AWKWARD APPROACH WAS MADE AS I WAITED FOR FRIENDS AT A THAI RESTAURANT ON POLK.

TABLE FOR TWO, PLEASE.

OH, I DON'T WORK HERE.

ON A LEVEL, THIS WAS *TERRIBLE*. BUT THE LOOK ON THEIR FACES MADE ME GO EASY ON THEM.

YOU CAN FIND THE HOST IN THE BACK.

...YEAH, UH, *THANKS*.

MISTAKES HAPPEN, AND PERHAPS THEY'VE LEARNED THAT NOT EVERY ASIAN PERSON IS HERE TO SERVE THEM.

BUT THEN, I NOTICE A BROKEN BUTTON ON MY SUIT, AND I'M SUDDENLY MORE SELF-CONSCIOUS OF MY OWN IMAGE.

TO THEM, I COULD'VE BEEN AN EARNEST HOST, SEEKING TO IMPRESS CUSTOMERS IN A BROKEN-DOWN SUIT.

WITH THE NEXT COUPLE WALKING THROUGH THE DOOR, I FOUND MYSELF JUMPING THE GUN.

HOST'S IN THE BACK.

I STARTED TO WORRY ABOUT SIGNALS IN OTHER ASPECTS OF MY LIFE AS WELL.

MY COUSIN, JAKYUNG, HAD GIVEN ME A PHONE MOUNT FOR DRIVING THAT I *DIDN'T* USE.

‹I WAS WONDERING IF YOU STILL HAD THAT GIFT.›

IT WAS HARD TO EXPLAIN THAT I DIDN'T WANT MORE STRANGERS RUNNING UP TO MY CAR, WHO'D SEE A PHONE MOUNTED ON THE DASHBOARD AS EVIDENCE THAT I WAS THEIR DRIVER.

I ALSO WONDERED IF A BETTER SUIT AND NECKTIE WOULD HELP.

MAYBE EVEN A *NICER* CAR.

BUT GIVEN THE FREQUENCY OF PAST INCIDENTS, I ALSO KNEW MORE EXPENSIVE STATUS SIGNIFIERS MIGHT ONLY MAKE ME LOOK LIKE AN UPGRADED VERSION OF *THE HELP.*

PARTICULARLY FOR PEOPLE WHO COULDN'T DISTINGUISH BETWEEN SERVICE AND SERVITUDE.

AHEM.

DOOR'S NOT GOING TO OPEN ITSELF, IS IT?

IN THE END, NONE OF THIS WAS REALLY ABOUT A BROKEN BUTTON.

THE MOST EXTREME INCIDENT HAPPENED WHILE STUCK DURING RUSH HOUR IN THE FINANCIAL DISTRICT.

THE DEMAND FOR EYE CONTACT COULD BE FELT ACROSS THE STREET WITH VIGOROUS HAND-WAVING AND A YELP FOR RECOGNITION.

AS THIS STRANGER CROSSED A BUSY LANE OF TRAFFIC TO REACH MY CAR, I FELT TRAPPED IN AN ACCIDENT UNFOLDING IN SLOW-MOTION.

TAP! TAP!

THEN, THINGS ACCELERATED QUICKLY WITH SUCCESSIVE TAPS AND A DEMAND:

COULD YOU POP YOUR TRUNK?

GET AWAY FROM MY CAR!

THE WORDS, WRAPPED IN *FIRE AND FURY*, SPILLED OUT OF ME.

ew!

MOMENTARILY STUNNED, THE STRANGER'S FACE THEN CONTORTED INTO INDIGNATION.

AND THE LAST WORD WAS THE DULL THUD OF A BAG BEING SLAMMED AGAINST THE HOOD.

THUMP

AS I LEAPT OUT OF MY CAR, I REALIZED THE FUTILITY OF MY MOVEMENT AS THE STRANGER RAN BACK ACROSS THE STREET.

HEY!

I COULDN'T ABANDON MY CAR IN THE MIDDLE OF DOWNTOWN TRAFFIC.

BUT THE "EW" AND VIOLENT BACKLASH STAYED WITH ME.

RETHINKING MY OWN RESPONSE, I COULDN'T REMEMBER THE LAST TIME I HAD YELLED AT SOMEONE LIKE THIS.

WHILE I DIDN'T FEEL GUILTY FOR PUSHING BACK, I DIDN'T FEEL VINDICATED EITHER.

ALL I HAD TO SHOW FOR IT WAS EXTRA ABUSE TO MY CAR.

YEARS PASSED.

I KEPT WORKING AT THE SAME NONPROFIT, BUILDING MY RESEARCH AND WRITING SKILLS.

AFTER 2015, UNSOLICITED APPROACHES TO MY CAR BECAME LESS FREQUENT, BUT THEN I ENCOUNTERED A VERY DIFFERENT KIND OF PROFESSIONAL APPROACH.

AFTER OFFICE-RELATED WORK THROUGHOUT THE DAY, WORK CONVERSATIONS WOULD GO ON AT NIGHT OVER DRINKS.

IN BARS, COLLEAGUES FROM OTHER NONPROFITS AND GOVERNMENT AGENCIES SWAPPED STORIES ABOUT THE HISTORY AND RELATIONSHIPS THAT UNDERGIRDED POLICY.

REMINDED OF MY FAMILY'S STORE, I FELT AT EASE BEING SURROUNDED BY BOTTLES LINING THE SHELVES.

PLUS, I APPRECIATED THE WORK AND CREATIVITY IN MIXING A GOOD DRINK.

THANKS, PLEASE KEEP THE CHANGE.

OVER SEVERAL BAR CHATS, I LEARNED PLENTY OF CONTEXT FOR MY WORK FROM GUILLERMO RODRIGUEZ.

GUILLERMO HAD A VARIED PROFESSIONAL BACKGROUND.

HE HAD LED NONPROFITS AND CITY DEPARTMENTS FOCUSED ON ENVIRONMENTAL POLICY AND JOB TRAINING.

WHICH PROMPTED HIS SUGGESTION ABOUT MY NEXT CAREER STEP:

SO HOW ABOUT TAKING OVER THE NONPROFIT?

...AS THE *EXECUTIVE DIRECTOR?*

MY FAMILY DOESN'T EVEN UNDERSTAND WHAT I DO AS A NONPROFIT ATTORNEY.

BEING AN EXECUTIVE DIRECTOR IS MORE ABOUT REVENUE AND MANAGING STAFF... YOUR PARENTS CAN THINK OF IT LIKE RUNNING A SMALL BUSINESS.

LOOK, THE ORGANIZATION WILL COLLAPSE WITHOUT A CHANGE IN DIRECTION. FUNDERS MAY BE EXCITED ABOUT THE TRANSITION WITH YOU AS *E.D.*

PLUS, I'LL DO SOMETHING I'VE NEVER DONE BEFORE FOR THIS NONPROFIT...

GUILLERMO SAVED HIS BEST ARGUMENT FOR LAST:

I'LL STEP ONTO THE BOARD.

YOU'LL HAVE *A LOT* OF FRIENDS TO HELP.

AS GOOD AS GUILLERMO WAS WITH DISPENSING STRATEGIC ADVICE, I KNEW IF THINGS WENT WRONG, I'D BE THE ONE RESPONSIBLE.

I KEPT A POKER FACE AS I THOUGHT CAREFULLY ABOUT THE EXTRA WORK IN RUNNING AN ORGANIZATION.

I HADN'T BEEN LOOKING FOR AN OPPORTUNITY LIKE THIS, BUT IT SEEMED EXCITING ENOUGH.

THINK ABOUT IT.

YOU'LL HAVE ALL THE SUPPORT THAT YOU NEED...

...IT WON'T BE THAT MUCH WORK.

THE ALEMBIC
READ, DRINK, EAT THINK
Take Your Time
415.

JULY 2015

MUCH OF THE EARLY DAYS OF RUNNING A NONPROFIT WAS RUNNING AROUND...

...AND FILLING OUT PAPERWORK.

NEXT TIME, I CAN OVERNIGHT THESE TO YOU.

NO WORRIES, LISA...WE SAVE ON POSTAGE THIS WAY.

LISA LE WAS OUR NONPROFIT'S CERTIFIED PUBLIC ACCOUNTANT.

SHE PREPARED THE FORMS THAT KEPT THE NONPROFIT IN GOOD LEGAL STANDING.

SEE YOU LATER!

WHILE LISA TOOK LOTS OF WORK OFF MY PLATE...

HUFF...

...HUFF...

...HUFF...

I COULD ONLY DO SO MUCH ON FOOT. ONCE AGAIN, MY CAR BECAME BOTH *STRESSFUL* AND *USEFUL* TO MY WORK.

FOR INSTANCE, MY CAR NEEDED A SPECIAL PERMIT TO PARK ON THE STREET NEAR MY OFFICE.

THURSDAY STREET CLEANING
1 HOUR PARKING 8AM TO 10PM EVERYDAY
EXCEPT VEHICLES WITH AREA U PERMIT

OTHERWISE, I WOULD BE RISKING *TICKETS* IF I DIDN'T MOVE MY CAR AFTER AN HOUR.

brightline DEFENSE
brightline DEFENSE

IN THEORY, AN HOUR OR TWO WAS ENOUGH TIME TO CHAT WITH PEOPLE IN THE OFFICE...

...LIKE AASTHA, A HIGH SCHOOL STUDENT WHO WAS ONE OF OUR EARLIEST VOLUNTEERS.

EDDIE, YOU GOT A PHONE MESSAGE!

IT'S ON A STICKY NOTE AT YOUR DESK.

brigh

GOT IT, THANKS!

BUT THEN, I WOULD BE SUCKED INTO A VORTEX OF EMAIL...

SO MUCH FOR *TL;DR*...I GUESS I NEED TO RESPOND TO THIS NOW.

...THEN SOME PHONE CALLS...

SO WHEN DO YOU THINK PAYMENT WILL BE ISSUED?

...THEN MORE EMAIL...

DID YOU EAT LUNCH, EDDIE?

NOT YET, AASTHA, BUT THANKS FOR THE REMINDER.

85

...THEN A MEETING ABOUT OUR JOB TRAINING PROGRAM WITH OTHER NONPROFITS AT OUR OFFICE.

OK, I TALKED WITH GIL AND HE'S PLANNING TO BUILD TOOLBOXES WITH THE YOUTH.

EDDIE WILL GET SUPPLIES AND SNACKS FOR THE CLASS TOO.

AND THEN JUST AS IT WAS TIME TO GO MOVE MY CAR...

RING RING

HI, THIS IS EDDIE.

OH, *HEY.*

YEAH, I WATCHED THE HEARING...

AND SO THE HOURS BECAME A BLUR...

WHEW.

...UNTIL THE SUDDEN REALIZATION THAT I HAD FORGOTTEN SOMETHING IN MY OWN LIFE.

MY CAR!

BECAUSE OF ENDLESS OFFICE WORK, MY CAR BECAME VULNERABLE TO TICKETS FOR OVERSTAYING THE NEIGHBORHOOD'S TIME-LIMITED RESTRICTIONS ON STREET PARKING.

I BEGAN TO DREAD SEEING THAT SLIP OF PAPER NESTLED UNDER THE WINDSHIELD WIPER.

I WOULD COMMUTE BY BUS OR BIKE WHEN I KNEW MY ENTIRE DAY WOULD BE PAPERWORK, BUT MY SCHEDULE WAS RARELY THAT PREDICTABLE.

BUILDING IN-DEPTH RELATIONSHIPS USUALLY MEANT MORE MEETINGS IN-PERSON.

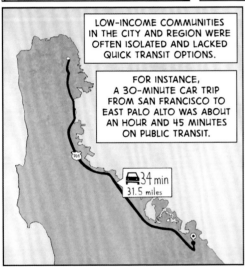

LOW-INCOME COMMUNITIES IN THE CITY AND REGION WERE OFTEN ISOLATED AND LACKED QUICK TRANSIT OPTIONS.

FOR INSTANCE, A 30-MINUTE CAR TRIP FROM SAN FRANCISCO TO EAST PALO ALTO WAS ABOUT AN HOUR AND 45 MINUTES ON PUBLIC TRANSIT.

34 min
31.5 miles

AFTER DRIVING SO MUCH ON ROUGHER ROADS, I BECAME USED TO FLAT TIRES.

REPLACING A TIRE WAS AN ACCEPTABLE COST IN ORDER TO SAVE HOURS ON COMMUTING.

ESPECIALLY IF I HAD TO ATTEND A GOVERNMENT OR COMMUNITY MEETING LATE INTO THE NIGHT.

USING PUBLIC TRANSIT AFTERWARD COULD THEN STRETCH A COMMUTE TO MUCH MORE THAN TWO HOURS.

MY CAR WAS THE ONLY REALISTIC WAY I COULD GET TO BED BY 2 OR 3 A.M.

Z

I DIDN'T MIND CRASHING AND BURNING AFTER A LONG WORKDAY AND NIGHT...

...BUT MY NONPROFIT'S NEED FOR MOBILITY STILL FORCED CHOICES BETWEEN SAVING TIME AND MONEY.

A $76 TICKET BECAME ANOTHER ACCEPTABLE COST OF BUSINESS.

THE ACCUMULATION OF COSTS LED TO WILD FANTASIES OF BLOWING UP THIS UNHEALTHY DYNAMIC.

OBLIVIOUS TO THIS, AN ENVIRONMENTAL ADVOCATE ONCE URGED ME TO SWITCH TO AN ELECTRIC VEHICLE IN 2019.

AS SIMPLY AS POSSIBLE, I EXPLAINED WHY I *COULDN'T*.

I GOT STUDENT LOANS, SO I JUST GET BY ON WHAT I HAVE.

EVEN AS THE HEAD OF MY NONPROFIT, MY SALARY DIDN'T COVER THE INTEREST ON MY LOANS.

BUT THERE'S A *$7,500* FEDERAL TAX CREDIT...

THIS EARNEST ARGUMENTATION WASN'T PERSUASIVE, AS I KNEW THE TAX CREDIT WAS ONLY A FRACTION OF THE PRICE.

I TRIED MAKING MY POINT AGAIN IN A GENTLE WAY.

I STILL HAVE TO MAKE NEW CAR PAYMENTS, RIGHT?

WHICH ONLY LED TO MORE OF THE SAME.

...BUT THERE'S ALSO A *STATE* EV REBATE...

AS THIS PERSON CONTINUED TO INSIST ON A NEW CAR I COULDN'T AFFORD, I FELT LIKE I WAS BEING FORCE-FED ENVIRONMENTALISM.

AFTER ALL, THE ONLY NEW BATTERY-POWERED DEVICE I COULD AFFORD WAS A CORDLESS VACUUM.

Click! Click!

AWW, COME ON, SHELLY.

WHO'S SHELLY?

DILINI WAS THE NEW STAFF ATTORNEY FOR OUR NONPROFIT.

SHE TOOK UP OUR ENVIRONMENTAL POLICY WORK AND LEGAL FILINGS...

...FREEING UP MY TIME FOR OTHER TASKS AND CREATIVE THINKING.

SHELLY IS THE NAME OF OUR NEW VACUUM.

OH.

WHY IS IT NAMED SHELLY?

FORTUNATELY, SHE ALSO DIDN'T THINK I WAS A LUNATIC FOR NAMING THE VACUUM CLEANER.

BECAUSE IT LOOKS LIKE A SHELL.

WHADDYA THINK?

OH, SURE.

WHILE DILINI HANDLED A LOT OF THE OFFICE WORK OF AN ATTORNEY, OUR NONPROFIT ALSO RAN JOB TRAINING PROGRAMS.

OUR JOB TRAINING PROGRAMS WOULD START WITH COMMUNITY OUTREACH AND PAPERWORK TO FIGURE OUT BARRIERS TO EMPLOYMENT.

...LET US KNOW IF YOU NEED A *DRIVER'S LICENSE*. WE CAN HELP YOU GET ONE.

DANIELA, OUR NONPROFIT'S PROGRAM COORDINATOR, WOULD SPEND DOZENS OF HOURS CORRALLING OTHER NONPROFIT, GOVERNMENT, AND COMPANY PARTNERS TO ADDRESS THESE BARRIERS.

OUR PROGRAMS OFTEN FOCUSED ON CONSTRUCTION, SINCE ONE COULD EARN DECENT WAGES AND BENEFITS WHILE WORKING ON A JOB SITE AS AN APPRENTICE.

DANIELA SCHEDULED A WIDE RANGE OF SERVICES FOR TRAINEES, INCLUDING CLASSROOM INSTRUCTION...

...CONSTRUCTION SITE VISITS...

...AND MOST IMPORTANTLY, PROJECTS THAT INVOLVED HANDS-ON TRAINING AND TOOLS OF THE TRADE.

WE WOULD BEGIN WITH RELATIVELY SIMPLE SKILLS WITH A HAMMER AND NAIL.

GREAT. LET THE WEIGHT OF THE HAMMER DO THE WORK.

HELL YEAH, I'M *BOB THE BUILDER!*

ONCE STUDENTS MASTERED DRIVING IN A NAIL STRAIGHT...

...THEY WOULD BUILD A MORE COMPLICATED PROJECT, SUCH AS A TOOLBOX...

...LEAVING THEM WITH A FEELING OF ACCOMPLISHMENT.

IT TOOK AN EXTRAORDINARY AMOUNT OF COORDINATION, BUT WE WERE PLACING THEM ON PATHWAYS TO SUSTAINABLE CAREERS.

DANIELA WOULD KEEP SERVICES RUNNING ON TIME.

EDDIE, WE RAN OUT OF SNACKS.

CAN YOU GET SOMETHING OTHER THAN GRANOLA?

AH, I'LL GO TO THE CLOSEST STORE.

GRANOLA'S INEXPENSIVE AND HEALTHIER THAN *CHIPS.*

BESIDES, THIS PROGRAM DOESN'T GET REIMBURSED FOR FOOD BY OUR FUNDING AGENCY, AND WE'RE RUNNING OUT OF MONEY...

...BUT OK, I'LL LOOK INTO IT.

DURING THESE EARLY DAYS, WE CONSTANTLY MADE SACRIFICES TO KEEP RUNNING THIS JOB TRAINING PROGRAM.

YEARS LATER, I LEARN MORE ABOUT MY GRANDFATHER WHILE GOING OVER HIS PAPERS.

HE WROTE ABOUT SMALL DETAILS OF HIS EARLY ADULT YEARS DURING WARTIME, LIKE HAVING COFFEE FOR THE FIRST TIME EVER FROM AN EMERGENCY SUPPLY PACKAGE...

난 항상 니편이야

...A DETAIL BETWEEN SENTENCES ABOUT SEEING DEAD SOLDIERS AS WELL AS A BOMBING ATTACK THAT KILLED THE WRONG PEOPLE.

HE REMEMBERED "BLACK COFFEE" SO STRONGLY THAT HE WROTE IT IN ENGLISH *TWICE*.

MY GRANDFATHER ALSO RECOUNTED HIS EFFORTS TO REBUILD SOUTH KOREA AND A SPECIFIC ELEMENTARY SCHOOL.

TRAVELING BY PLANE, GENERAL EISENHOWER INSPECTED THE SCHOOL AND LATER ARRANGED FOR MORE RECONSTRUCTION AID FOR RURAL REGIONS THROUGHOUT SOUTH KOREA, WHICH WEREN'T WIDELY COVERED BY THE MEDIA.

I BRING THIS UP WITH MY MOM, AND SHE'S *NOT IMPRESSED*.

⟨YAH, YOUR GRANDFATHER WAS A PATRIOT AND WAS VERY SUCCESSFUL FOR SOME TIME.⟩

BUT HE COULD BE *STUPID* TOO.

MY MOTHER ALTERNATED BETWEEN ENGLISH AND ⟨KOREAN⟩ TO EXPLAIN.

HE HAD THIS CLASSMATE, A PROFESSOR FROM SEOUL NATIONAL UNIVERSITY, THAT HE INVESTED IN.

⟨I REMEMBER, EVERY MORNING, HE CAME TO SEE YOUR GRANDFATHER FOR MORE MONEY.⟩

THOK! THOK!

⟨BUT YOUR GRANDMOTHER *KNEW*. SHE WARNED HIM: "DON'T TRUST HIM."⟩

HE GAVE HIM MORE MONEY ANYWAYS.

THOK! THOK!

YOUR GRANDFATHER WOULD ALSO GUARANTEE SOMEONE ELSE'S LOANS WITH OUR HOUSE, AND HE LOST OUR HOME BECAUSE THEY DEFAULTED.

<WHY DOESN'T HE KNOW THAT HE WAS USED BY SOMEONE?>

ALL THOSE *STUPID* THINGS, MAKING YOUR GRANDMOTHER SUFFER...

<...AND THEIR FOUR CHILDREN--*YOUR AUNTS AND ME*--SUFFERED TOO!>

AS SHE SAID THIS, MY MOM CHOPPED MORE FURIOUSLY.

THOK! THOK! THOK! THOK! THOK!

EVEN IF HE COMES BACK NOW...

...I DON'T THINK I WOULD FORGIVE HIM FOR WHAT HE DID.

<WHY DO YOU CARE SO MUCH ABOUT GRANDFATHER?>

OH...JUST CURIOUS.

TRUTH BE TOLD, I SEE MORE OF MYSELF IN THESE PAGES THAN I'D LIKE.

MY PARENTS PURSUED ECONOMIC SUCCESS, BUILT OVER TIME BY SELLING BOTTLES WRAPPED IN BAGS.

AND THEN REINVESTED WHAT THEY HAD IN *ME*.

WHICH MAKES NONPROFIT WORK EVEN MORE DIFFICULT FOR ME.

IT'S ALWAYS BEEN HARD NOT TO WORRY ABOUT MY PARENTS.

WHO HAVE SACRIFICED SO MUCH FOR ME TO ACHIEVE A LAW DEGREE.

THE IRONY OF FEELING SELFISH FOR PURSUING NONPROFIT WORK OVER THE YEARS DOESN'T ESCAPE ME.

WOULD YOU LIKE A BAG FOR AN EXTRA 25 CENTS?

I SUPPOSE THERE'S A PRICE FOR EVERYTHING.

NAH, I'M GOOD.

THANK YOU.

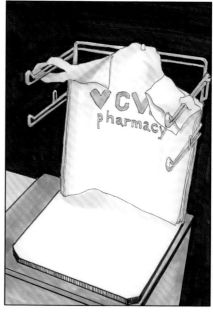

CHAPTER FOUR

MAMA JACKSON'S SWORD

JANUARY 2015

RING! RING!

DR. ESPANOLA JACKSON ALWAYS SEEMED TO BE READY AT THE PHONE.

HELLO?

HELLO, MAMA. IT'S EDDIE AHN...IS NOW STILL A GOOD TIME TO STOP BY?

YES, I'LL BE HOME.

RUNNING THE NONPROFIT WAS ALL-CONSUMING.

STILL, WHEN I COULD GET AWAY, I WOULD VISIT ESPANOLA.

AND I TRIED TO BRING SOMETHING SPECIAL EACH TIME.

Fresh Flowers

ESPANOLA'S COMMUNITY WAS BAYVIEW—HUNTERS POINT.

GETTING TO HER HOME FROM THE OFFICE COULD BE A SHORT OR LONG TRIP.

SOUTH 101 San Jose

WITH LIGHT TRAFFIC ON US 101, IT WAS ABOUT A 10-MINUTE DRIVE.

BY BUS OR LIGHT RAIL, IT WOULD TYPICALLY TAKE AN HOUR.

TRANSIT ISOLATION WAS ONE OF MANY ISSUES THAT DEFINED THE COMMUNITY.

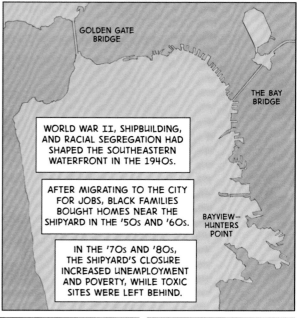

GOLDEN GATE BRIDGE

THE BAY BRIDGE

WORLD WAR II, SHIPBUILDING, AND RACIAL SEGREGATION HAD SHAPED THE SOUTHEASTERN WATERFRONT IN THE 1940s.

AFTER MIGRATING TO THE CITY FOR JOBS, BLACK FAMILIES BOUGHT HOMES NEAR THE SHIPYARD IN THE '50s AND '60s.

BAYVIEW— HUNTERS POINT

IN THE '70s AND '80s, THE SHIPYARD'S CLOSURE INCREASED UNEMPLOYMENT AND POVERTY, WHILE TOXIC SITES WERE LEFT BEHIND.

ESPANOLA'S JOURNEY REFLECTED THIS HISTORY: IN 1943, SHE CAME TO SAN FRANCISCO FROM TEXAS, AND IN 1968, SHE BOUGHT HER HOME IN THE BAYVIEW.

SHE REMAINED HERE FOR DECADES, HOLDING IT DOWN.

THIS WAS HER COMMUNITY, HER FAMILY.

THANK YOU, BABY.

ESPANOLA WOULD SHARE THE ORAL HISTORY OF HER ENVIRONMENTAL JUSTICE WORK.

AS ONE OF *THE BIG FIVE,* ELOISE WOULD...

EVEN THOUGH NOT IN FULL HEALTH WHEN I VISITED, SHE TOOK GREAT JOY GOING OVER PAST AND FUTURE STRUGGLES:

FROM FIGHTING AGAINST FOSSIL FUEL POWER PLANTS SITED IN LOW-INCOME COMMUNITIES...

...TO FIGHTING FOR SOLAR ON LOW-INCOME HOMES AND APARTMENT BUILDINGS.

IN CONTRAST, MY GRANDFATHER NEVER TOLD ME HIS STORIES. WE INSTEAD SHARED *WRITTEN* HISTORIES: ENGLISH-LANGUAGE MAGAZINES AND BOOKS HE HAD COLLECTED FOR HIMSELF.

WHEN I VISITED SOUTH KOREA AS A CHILD, I WOULD SPEND HOURS WITH HIS MATERIALS.

WE SHARED AN UNSPOKEN BOND THROUGH PAGES OF POPULAR SCIENCE CONTENT AND WEIRD FACTOIDS.

99

AS I SPENT HOURS LISTENING TO ESPANOLA'S ORAL HISTORY, SHE SAID SOMETHING ABOUT THE FUTURE THAT STUCK WITH ME.

YES, THERE'S *ALWAYS* MORE WORK AHEAD.

THAT'S WHY I SPEND SO MUCH TIME TEACHING, GETTING THEM TO *PICK UP THE SWORD.*

FOR THE NEXT VISIT, I BROUGHT DILINI, OUR NONPROFIT'S STAFF ATTORNEY.

INITIALLY, I WAS WORRIED ABOUT DILINI NOT HITTING IT OFF WITH ESPANOLA.

STILL, STEPPING BACK TO ALLOW RELATIONSHIPS TO GROW...

PLEASE GO IN WITHOUT ME. I'M GONNA MAKE A CALL.

SOUNDS GOOD.

...WAS PROBABLY ONE OF THE BETTER DECISIONS I'VE EVER MADE.

GOT SOME HOMEWORK, I SEE.

YEAH, A LETTER TO DRAFT...

TO KEEP THE LIGHTS ON, I SPENT A LOT OF TIME WORKING THROUGH BILLS SUCH AS RENT, UTILITIES, AND PRINTING.

GIVEN THIS OVERHEAD, I SAVED ON COSTS BY BEING THE OFFICE SECRETARY.

I MADE COPIES OF YOUR LETTER DRAFT FOR ESPANOLA!

TELL MAMA I SAID HELLO.

I DIDN'T MIND, AS THERE WAS COMFORT IN THE ROUTINE OF PAPERWORK.

HI, THIS IS EDDIE...IS NOW A GOOD TIME TO STOP BY?

BUT I LEARNED TO NOT GET *TOO* COMFORTABLE...

NO, I'M SORRY...SOMETHING HAPPENED. SHE'S IN THE HOSPITAL.

IS IT OK IF I COME TO THE HOSPITAL?

...OK, WHAT'S THE ADDRESS?

AS THINGS COULD QUICKLY CHANGE FOR THE WORSE.

FROM MY EYE SURGERY DAYS, I WAS USED TO HOSPITALS BY NOW.

BUT IT WAS STILL HARD TO SEE ESPANOLA CONFINED TO BED.

HEY, MAMA. HOW ARE YOU FEELING?

SHE DIDN'T MISS A BEAT THOUGH.

LISTEN, DID YOU TAKE A LOOK AT THAT LAND?

THIS DIDN'T SURPRISE ME...I HAD FOUND FLOWERS IN HER PREFERRED COLOR, *PURPLE*...

...AND I HAD ANOTHER GIFT READY.

GOT DILINI'S DRAFT FOR YOU...

THERE WAS A GLIMMER OF RECOGNITION.

WHAT DID SURPRISE ME WAS THAT ESPANOLA DIDN'T REACH FOR THE LETTER. INSTEAD, SHE KEPT ON TALKING IN A LOW, STEADY VOICE.

THE FACILITY, TO TAKE A LOOK AT THAT TOO...

AND I REALIZED SHE DIDN'T NEED THE LETTER, FLOWERS, OR MUCH ELSE.

...AND I *TOLD* THEM, THEY NEED TO--

SHE JUST NEEDED SOMEONE TO LISTEN.

SO I STAYED AWHILE LONGER, JUST TO LISTEN.

THIS WOULD BE THE LAST TIME I WOULD SEE ESPANOLA ALIVE.

LATER ON, GUILLERMO AND I WOULD TALK ABOUT ESPANOLA OVER DRINKS.

A LOT OF PEOPLE THINK THEY CAN PARACHUTE INTO THE COMMUNITY AND WORK WITH SOMEONE LIKE ESPANOLA.

BUT THEY UNDERESTIMATED HOW SHE WOULD SIZE THEM UP.

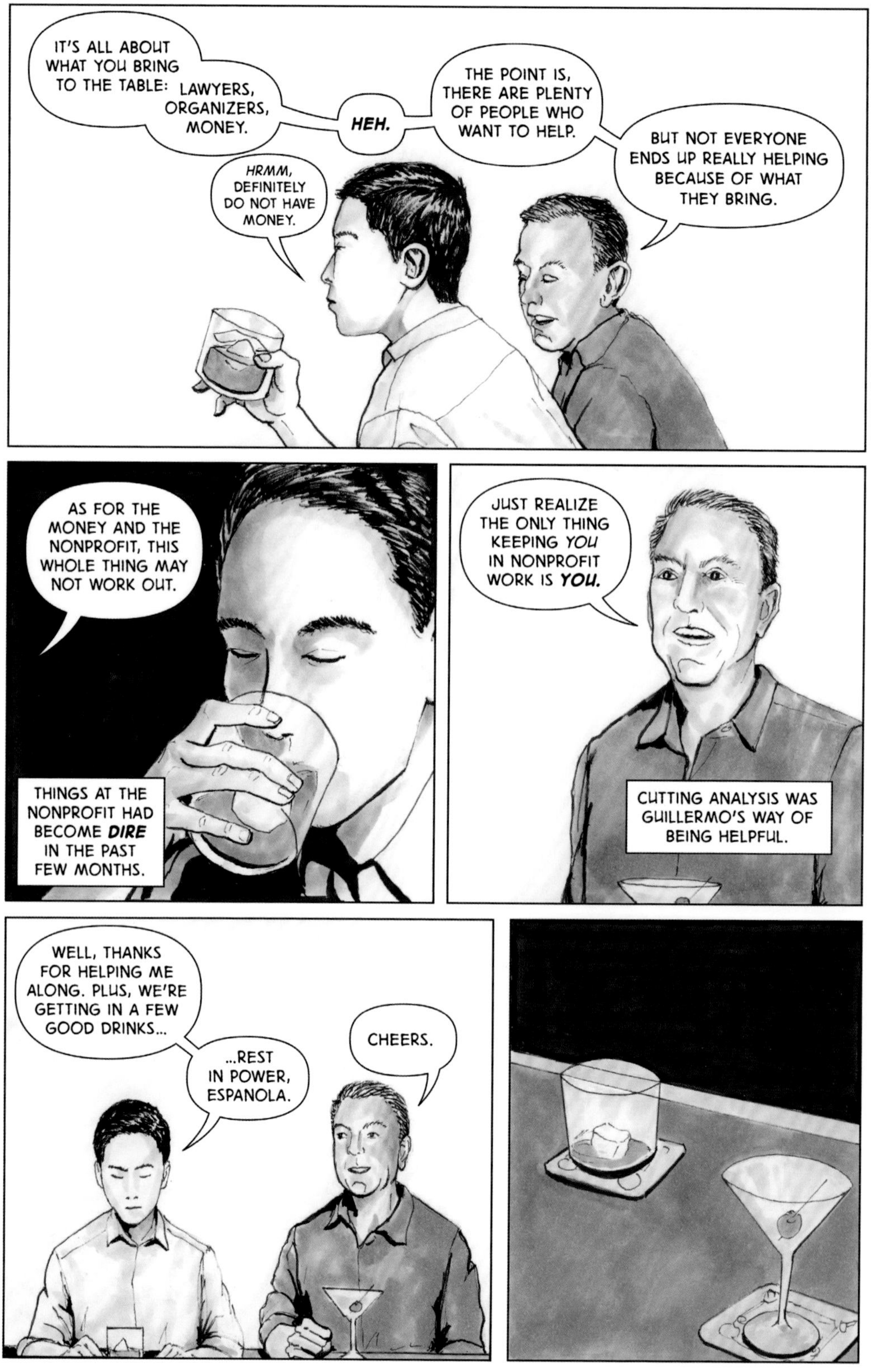
IT'S ALL ABOUT WHAT YOU BRING TO THE TABLE: LAWYERS, ORGANIZERS, MONEY.
HEH.
THE POINT IS, THERE ARE PLENTY OF PEOPLE WHO WANT TO HELP.
BUT NOT EVERYONE ENDS UP REALLY HELPING BECAUSE OF WHAT THEY BRING.
HRMM, DEFINITELY DO NOT HAVE MONEY.
AS FOR THE MONEY AND THE NONPROFIT, THIS WHOLE THING MAY NOT WORK OUT.
THINGS AT THE NONPROFIT HAD BECOME ***DIRE*** IN THE PAST FEW MONTHS.
JUST REALIZE THE ONLY THING KEEPING *YOU* IN NONPROFIT WORK IS ***YOU.***
CUTTING ANALYSIS WAS GUILLERMO'S WAY OF BEING HELPFUL.
WELL, THANKS FOR HELPING ME ALONG. PLUS, WE'RE GETTING IN A FEW GOOD DRINKS...
...REST IN POWER, ESPANOLA.
CHEERS.

WHEN ESPANOLA PASSED IN 2016, SO MANY PEOPLE WANTED TO MEMORIALIZE HER THAT THERE WERE **MULTIPLE** SERVICES.

I ENJOYED BEING A QUIET PRESENCE IN THE BACK...

...AND WE ALL KNOW SHE'D *FIGHT* FOR US--

YES, THAT'S RIGHT!

...LISTENING TO TESTIMONIALS ABOUT A LIFE WELL-LIVED...

...AND REMINDING MYSELF HOW I WAS JUST A SMALL PART OF HER WORLD.

COMMUNITY WORK SHOULD NEVER BE ABOUT MY OWN EGO.

IT WASN'T SO MUCH ABOUT PICKING UP **ESPANOLA'S** SWORD...

...AS MUCH AS IT WAS *INSPIRING OTHERS* TO PICK UP THE SWORD.

AFTER ESPANOLA'S SERVICE, I THOUGHT A LOT ABOUT WHAT I WOULD SHARE ABOUT ESPANOLA, AND HOW I WOULD CREATE MY OWN CELEBRATION FOR HER.

Celebrating the Life and Legacy of Mother & Dr. Espanola Jackson

Sunrise February 9, 1933

Sunset ... 2016

Espanola Has Been on the Battlefield for over 58 Years

I CONTINUED TO DEVELOP MY DRAWING SKILLS.

UGH, EARS ARE TRICKY...

AT THAT TIME, I DIDN'T THINK MY ARTISTIC ABILITIES WERE GOOD ENOUGH FOR HER STORIES.

I ALSO NEVER SEEMED TO HAVE ENOUGH TIME FOR ART SINCE THE NONPROFIT'S OPERATIONS AND PAPERWORK KEPT ME BUSY LATE INTO THE NIGHT.

brightline DEFENSE
helping communities sustainable communities

I DIDN'T MIND WORKING THESE LONG HOURS, AS I WANTED TO CARRY ON ESPANOLA'S SPIRIT OF SERVING THE COMMUNITY. *PLUS*, MY FAMILY'S WORK ETHIC WAS BAKED INTO MY PERSONALITY.

BUT FRIENDS LIKE LIZ AND PAULA, WHO WERE PSYCHIATRIC NURSE PRACTITIONERS, PUZZLED OVER *WHY* I CONTINUED WHEN MY WORK WAS EXCEEDINGLY DIFFICULT AND ISOLATING.

EDDIE, DO YOU EVER FEEL *ENTITLED*?

NAH.

WHILE MY FRIENDS GENERALLY UNDERSTOOD HOW MUCH I CARED ABOUT SERVICE TO OTHERS...

...*MY DAD* WAS THE HARDEST PERSON TO TALK TO ABOUT NONPROFIT WORK.

<...DESCRIBE TO ME WHAT YOU DO.>

WE WORK WITH ENVIRONMENTAL LAWS THAT CREATE CLEAN ENERGY AND LOCAL JOBS.

SO IT'S ABOUT *FINANCIAL* BENEFITS FOR ALL COMMUNITIES.

I SIMPLIFIED MY WORK'S DETAILS, FOCUSING ON ITS ECONOMIC ASPECTS.

OH.

<SO HOW MUCH MONEY ARE YOU MAKING?>

MY DAD'S FOCUS ON MONEY WAS MORE EXTREME THAN MY MOM'S.

AFTER THEIR LIQUOR STORE CLOSED, MY PARENTS DIVORCED, WHICH DEEPENED MY DAD'S ISOLATION.

AT HOME ALONE IN TEXAS, HE WOULD DRINK LEFTOVER INVENTORY FROM THE CLOSED STORE AND EAT EXCESSIVE AMOUNTS OF CHEESE AND CURED MEATS.

THESE FOOD SAMPLES WERE FROM HIS NEW EXPORT BUSINESS, AND HE OFTEN ASKED FOR LEGAL ADVICE.

<WHAT KIND OF LAWYER DOESN'T MAKE MONEY?>

I KNEW OUR PERSONALTIES WERE FAR TOO DIFFERENT TO WORK TOGETHER.

THOUGH WE DID SHARE A FEW THINGS IN COMMON...

...A LOVE FOR TRAVEL, FOR INSTANCE...

...SMALL COURTESIES FOR OTHERS...

HAVE A NICE DAY!

...AND FOR SOME TIME, I WORE MY DAD'S LEATHER JACKET.

WHILE HE SIMPLY SWITCHED TO ANOTHER COAT AND SEEMED UNSENTIMENTAL ABOUT IT...

...THAT OLD LEATHER COAT STILL INFLUENCES NEWER CLOTHING I WEAR NOW...

...AND EVEN SOME CHOICES I'VE MADE.

MAY 2017

ONE EARLY EVENING, AS I WALKED HOME FROM THE GYM...

GEARY

14TH AVE

A BMW SUV SIDLED UP NEXT TO ME WITH A PASSENGER LEANING OUT THE WINDOW.

MI SCUSI, EH...

WE HAVE NO INTERNET SERVICE, AND WE ARE LOST. HOW WE GET TO THE AIRPORT?

IT WAS ODD THAT THEY WERE ON THE OTHER SIDE OF TOWN, AWAY FROM THE HIGHWAYS THAT LED TO THE AIRPORT.

OH, WOW-- YOU'RE REALLY FAR AWAY.

BUT I TRIED MY BEST TO HELP.

OK, TURN RIGHT ON THIS STREET, AND THEN--

UNFORTUNATELY, I'D SOON KNOW THE MEANING OF THAT SAYING: "NO GOOD DEED..."

I, AH, THANK YOU FOR HELPING ME!

SURE, NO PROBLEM.

I GIVE YOU A GIFT!

WE ARE LEAVING SAN FRANCISCO AFTER A FASHION SHOW, AND WE HAVE A *PROBLEM.*

WE BRING LEATHER COATS BUT CAN NOT BRING THEM BACK TO ITALY WITHOUT--

--COME SI DICE...

EH, CUSTOM TAX. SO WE GIVE ONE TO YOU!

THE STORY WAS TOLD RAPIDLY IN CONFUSING FRAGMENTS.

OH, NO NEED.

I DIDN'T NEED ANOTHER LEATHER COAT, BUT THEY WERE VERY INSISTENT.

IT IS A *BIG* FAVOR TO US!

OR ELSE WE THROW AWAY, *VERY* WASTEFUL!

THEN QUICKLY JUMPING OUT THE CAR AND OPENING UP THE BACKSEAT, THE FASHIONISTA GESTURED CHEERFULLY.

COME! TRY ONE ON.

THEN YOU CAN GIVE TO A FRIEND!

THE WEIRDNESS OF THIS WAS OFFSET BY THE TORN DESIGNER JEANS, PRISTINE SNEAKERS, AND GOOFY GRIN.

YES, *YES!*

THE CAR'S PLUSH LEATHER INTERIOR DIDN'T REALLY GIVE OFF ABDUCTION VIBES.

THE OFFER SEEMED HARMLESS. I WOULD STEP IN FOR A QUICK LOOK, AND WITH THE DOOR OPEN, I COULD STEP OUT AT ANY TIME.

WHAT COULD *POSSIBLY* GO WRONG?

SLAM!

WITH THE DOOR SHUT BEHIND ME, I IMMEDIATELY LOOKED TO THE FRONT AND STUDIED THE DRIVER.

QUICKLY SLIDING INTO THE OTHER BACK SEAT, THE FASHIONISTA ANNOUNCED:

HE IS CLAUDIO...SAY HELLO!

CLAUDIO SAID NOTHING AS HIS GAZE BORDERED ON BOREDOM.

THE FASHIONISTA THEN PULLED OUT A COAT FROM A SET OF GARMENT BAGS.

I AM GIANNI, AND WE WORK FOR ARMANI IN MILAN.

THIS IS FOR A **NEW** LINE OF FASHION!

WITH A QUICK FLOURISH, GIANNI RAN A LIGHTER UP AND DOWN THE JACKET.

SEE? REAL LEATHER.

I WAS REMINDED OF MY DAD'S WORK IN EXPORTING AMERICAN FOOD PRODUCTS.

YEARS AGO, I HAD HELPED HIM OUT IN A TRADE SHOW, AND GIANNI'S PATTER MATCHED THE RELENTLESS ENERGY NEEDED TO EXPLAIN PRODUCT QUALITY.

AS I FOCUSED MY ENERGIES ON NONPROFIT WORK AND BECAME AN EXECUTIVE DIRECTOR, MY DAD HAD BECOME INCREASINGLY HOSTILE.

‹WHAT ARE YOU DOING WITH YOUR LIFE?›

‹EVEN AFTER GRADUATING LAW SCHOOL, YOU'RE STILL WORKING AS AN **INTERN**.›

BUT THIS COAT REPRESENTED SOMETHING DIFFERENT THAN MY DAD'S TRANSACTIONAL WORLDVIEW, WHERE THE ONLY METRIC OF SUCCESS WAS MONEY.

HERE WAS **PROOF** OF SHARED GENEROSITY AMONG STRANGERS, AND I COULD IMAGINE HIS REACTION...

GIANNI INTERRUPTED MY REVERIE WITH SOMETHING *MORE.*

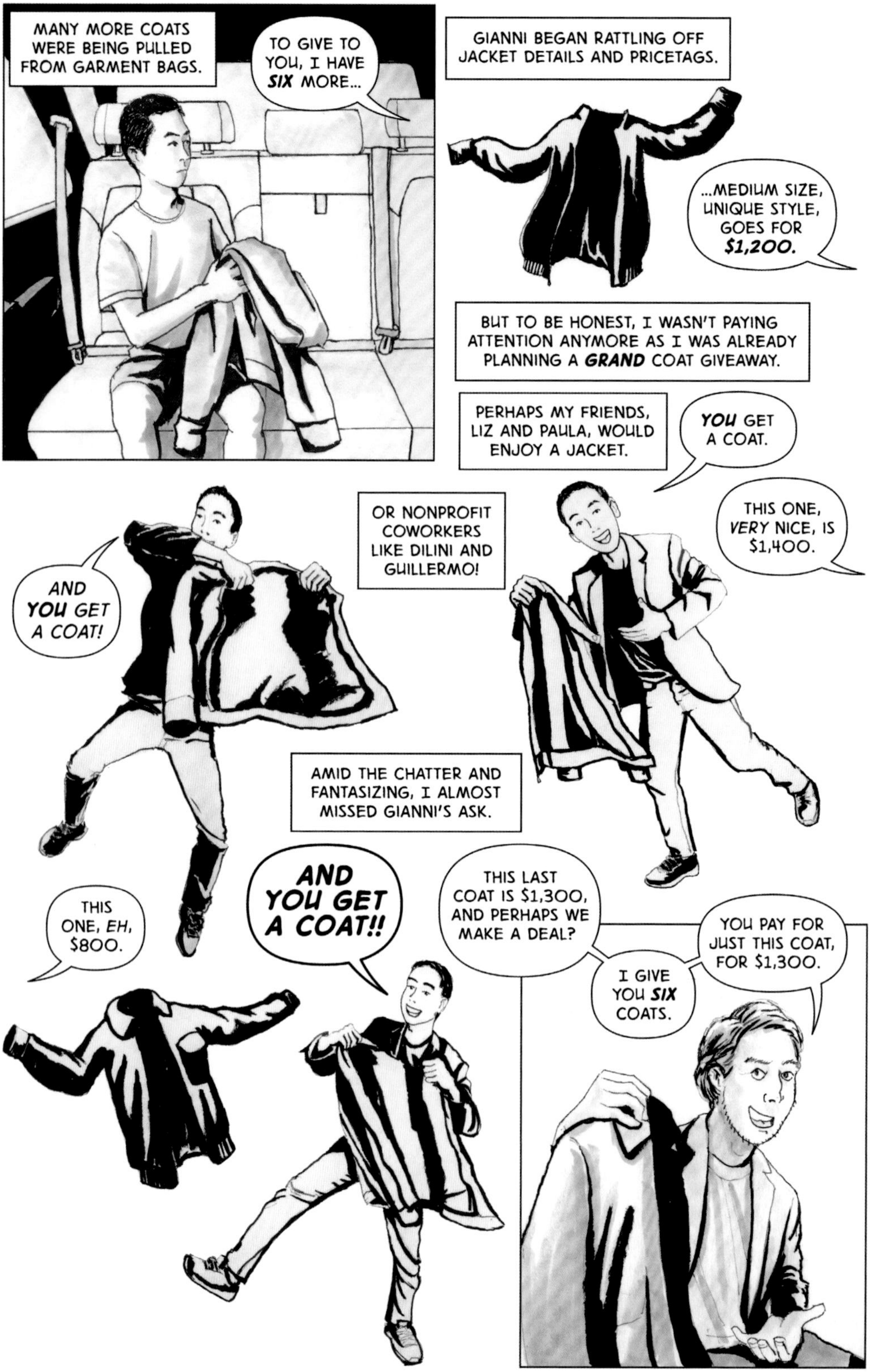
MANY MORE COATS WERE BEING PULLED FROM GARMENT BAGS.
TO GIVE TO YOU, I HAVE **SIX** MORE...
GIANNI BEGAN RATTLING OFF JACKET DETAILS AND PRICETAGS.
...MEDIUM SIZE, UNIQUE STYLE, GOES FOR **$1,200.**
BUT TO BE HONEST, I WASN'T PAYING ATTENTION ANYMORE AS I WAS ALREADY PLANNING A **GRAND** COAT GIVEAWAY.
PERHAPS MY FRIENDS, LIZ AND PAULA, WOULD ENJOY A JACKET.
YOU GET A COAT.
OR NONPROFIT COWORKERS LIKE DILINI AND GUILLERMO!
AND **YOU** GET A COAT!
THIS ONE, *VERY* NICE, IS $1,400.
AMID THE CHATTER AND FANTASIZING, I ALMOST MISSED GIANNI'S ASK.
THIS ONE, *EH*, $800.
AND YOU GET A COAT!!
THIS LAST COAT IS $1,300, AND PERHAPS WE MAKE A DEAL?
I GIVE YOU **SIX** COATS.
YOU PAY FOR JUST THIS COAT, FOR $1,300.

heh!

GIANNI DROPPED THE DOLLAR AMOUNT SO NONCHALANTLY THAT IT SEEMED LIKE A JOKE.

BUT THE BLANK STARE INDICATED OTHERWISE.

ohhh... YOU'RE NOT JOKING.

LITTLE DID GIANNI KNOW: MY PERSONAL FINANCES WERE WEIGHED DOWN BY LAW SCHOOL DEBT AND NONPROFIT WORK.

OH, NOT GOOD.

MY CHECKING ACCOUNT HAD DIPPED TO $8.88, WHICH MEANT MORE COST-CUTTING MEASURES.

HRMM, *REALLY* NOT GOOD.

THE *25-CENT* DIFFERENCE BETWEEN A BAKED BBQ BUN AND A STEAMED BUN HAD BECOME A LONG-TERM FINANCIAL DECISION FOR ME.

WHICH MADE FOR A FAST RESPONSE:

NOPE, CAN'T BUY ANY COATS.

BUT THEY ARE *VERY* NICE, PART OF A NEW LINE...

GIANNI SEEMED CLUELESS TO THE GROWING CHASM BETWEEN US.

GIORGIO ARMANI COULD HAVE PERSONALLY STITCHED THESE COATS BY HAND, BUT ALL I WAS THINKING WAS ABOUT MY NEXT CHAR SIU BAO.

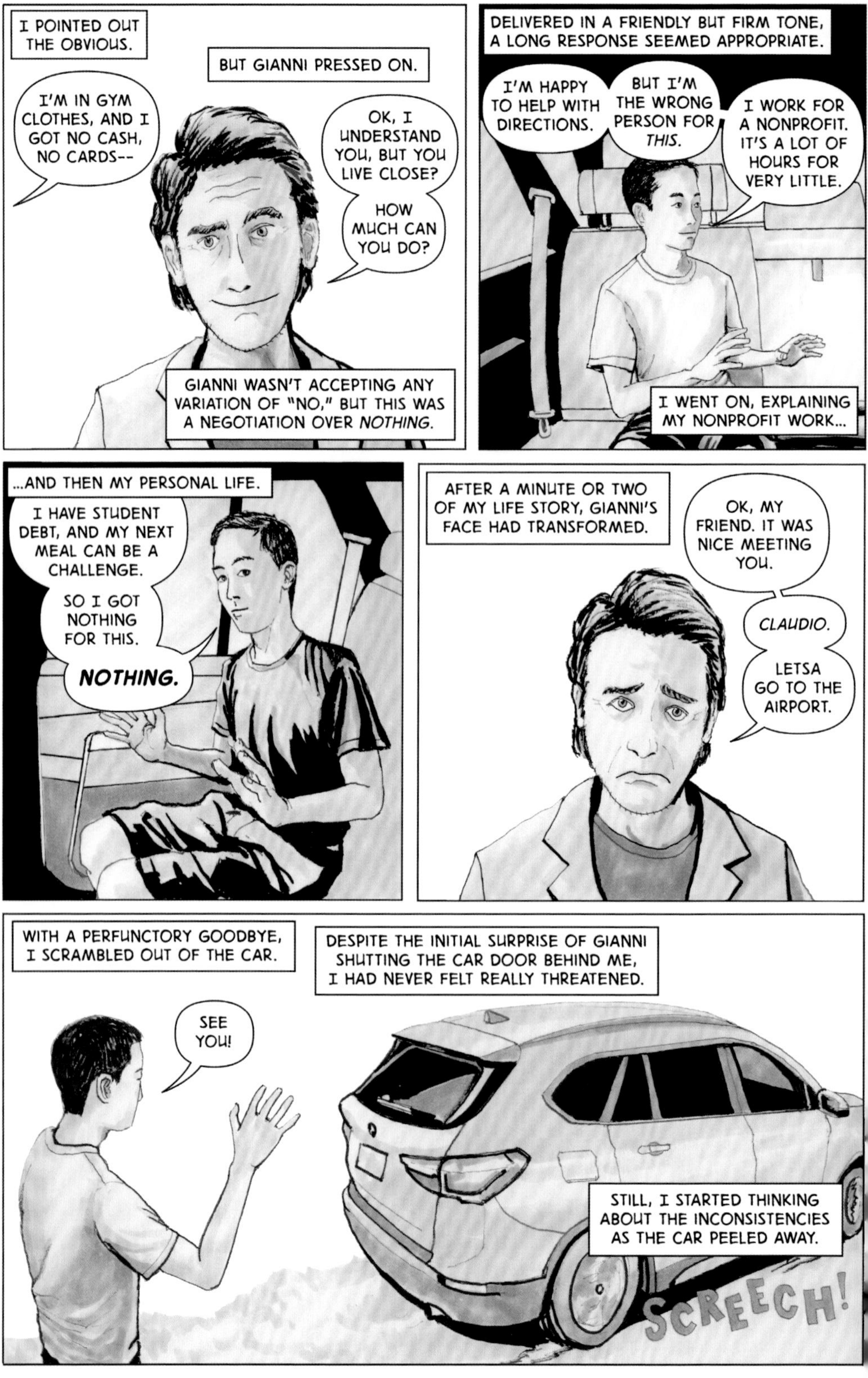
I POINTED OUT THE OBVIOUS.
I'M IN GYM CLOTHES, AND I GOT NO CASH, NO CARDS--
BUT GIANNI PRESSED ON.
OK, I UNDERSTAND YOU, BUT YOU LIVE CLOSE?
HOW MUCH CAN YOU DO?
GIANNI WASN'T ACCEPTING ANY VARIATION OF "NO," BUT THIS WAS A NEGOTIATION OVER *NOTHING*.
DELIVERED IN A FRIENDLY BUT FIRM TONE, A LONG RESPONSE SEEMED APPROPRIATE.
I'M HAPPY TO HELP WITH DIRECTIONS.
BUT I'M THE WRONG PERSON FOR *THIS*.
I WORK FOR A NONPROFIT. IT'S A LOT OF HOURS FOR VERY LITTLE.
I WENT ON, EXPLAINING MY NONPROFIT WORK...
...AND THEN MY PERSONAL LIFE.
I HAVE STUDENT DEBT, AND MY NEXT MEAL CAN BE A CHALLENGE.
SO I GOT NOTHING FOR THIS.
NOTHING.
AFTER A MINUTE OR TWO OF MY LIFE STORY, GIANNI'S FACE HAD TRANSFORMED.
OK, MY FRIEND. IT WAS NICE MEETING YOU.
CLAUDIO.
LETSA GO TO THE AIRPORT.
WITH A PERFUNCTORY GOODBYE, I SCRAMBLED OUT OF THE CAR.
DESPITE THE INITIAL SURPRISE OF GIANNI SHUTTING THE CAR DOOR BEHIND ME, I HAD NEVER FELT REALLY THREATENED.
SEE YOU!
STILL, I STARTED THINKING ABOUT THE INCONSISTENCIES AS THE CAR PEELED AWAY.
SCREECH!

A QUICK ONLINE SEARCH REVEALED MORE ABOUT THE PROCESS AND SCALE OF THE ARMANI HUSTLE, WHICH HAS BEEN HONED IN THE U.S., U.K., CANADA, AND AUSTRALIA.

I ALSO FOUND OUT THAT AN OLD FRIEND IN NEW YORK CITY HAD A SIMILAR EXPERIENCE.

THE GOAL IS TO PERSUADE THE TARGET TO PAY SEVERAL HUNDRED DOLLARS FOR COUNTERFEIT COATS THAT COST $20 TO $40 EACH.

TO THIS END, THE HUSTLERS CALIBRATE EACH INTERACTION, PLAYING OFF THE TARGET'S RESPONSE TO REQUESTS.

FOR INSTANCE, ASKING FOR DIRECTIONS TESTS THE TARGET'S AMENABILITY.

THE INVITATION TO STEP INSIDE THE CAR IS DESIGNED TO INCREASE THE FEELING OF COMMITMENT.

EVEN IF THE TARGET SIDESTEPS THAT TRAP, THEY CAN EXPLOIT ANY MIX OF EMOTIONS:

CONFUSION, EMPATHY, GREED, GRANDIOSITY.

NEVER INTIMIDATING, THEY INSTEAD CAJOLE AND CHARM THEIR WAY TO AN EXCHANGE.

I COULD IMAGINE "GIANNI" HUDDLING WITH AN ACTING COACH, PERFECTING THESE APPROACHES.

LISTEN, I GOT SOME COATS IN THE TRUNK. WANNA HAVE ONE?

A *GIFT* FROM ME TO YOU.

HM, TRY THAT AGAIN--WITH LESS *DE NIRO* AND MORE *ROBERTO BENIGNI*.

AT ANY RATE, KNOWING ALL THIS DETAIL HASN'T CHANGED MY GENERAL OUTLOOK ON LIFE.

NOT BECAUSE I HAVE DELUSIONS THAT A CASH-POOR EXISTENCE SOMEHOW TRIUMPHED OVER AN INTERNATIONAL CRIMINAL EMPIRE.

BUT BECAUSE MY PARENTS HAVE TAUGHT ME CERTAIN VALUES...

...SUCH AS BEING GENEROUS TO OTHERS...

...AND STAYING CURIOUS ABOUT THE WORLD.

(...THOUGH I'VE SINCE LEARNED TO NOT GO INSIDE A STRANGER'S CAR.)

I REMEMBER A SPECIFIC MOMENT AFTER MY LAW SCHOOL GRADUATION IN 2009.

DESPITE THE JOY OF THAT DAY, THE ECONOMY WAS IN TERRIBLE SHAPE, AND MANY LAW SCHOOL GRADUATES, INCLUDING MYSELF, WERE STRUGGLING TO FIND WORK.

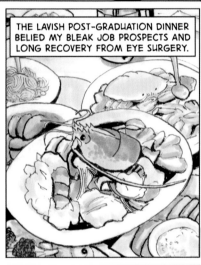

THE LAVISH POST-GRADUATION DINNER BELIED MY BLEAK JOB PROSPECTS AND LONG RECOVERY FROM EYE SURGERY.

BUT INSTEAD OF WORRYING ABOUT MY FUTURE, MY DAD LAUNCHED INTO A SURPRISING MONOLOGUE.

WELL, THE ECONOMY IS NOT EASY...

...BUT I AM NOT WORRIED.

PRAISE WAS NOT COMMON IN OUR FAMILY, AND IF GIVEN, IT WAS USUALLY CUT WITH SOME CRITICISM TO KEEP US HUMBLE.

EDDIE WORKS HARD AT WHATEVER HE DOES.

SO I THINK HE WILL BE SUCCESSFUL.

I KEPT WAITING FOR THE OTHER SHOE TO DROP.

. . .

AND HE HAS A NICE VOICE.

TAKEN ABACK BY THIS, I DIDN'T HAVE MUCH TO SAY.

OH, UH...

THANKS, *APPA.*

YEARS AFTER ENCOUNTERING THE ARMANI HUSTLE, I'D THINK ABOUT HOW MY DAD WOULD HAVE REACTED TO GIANNI.

EXCUSE ME, SIR.

HIS INITIAL RESPONSE PROBABLY WOULD HAVE BEEN GENEROUS, NOT FROM AN INABILITY TO READ PEOPLE.

WE'RE TRYING TO FIND PORTSMOUTH SQUARE. DO YOU KNOW WHERE IT IS?

BUT FROM UNDERSTANDING THAT GOOD CHEER AND PERSEVERANCE WERE HELPFUL CONSTANTS.

I THINK OF MY DAD CARRYING ON, EVEN AS THINGS FELL APART FOR HIM.

AND THAT'S ENOUGH FOR ME TO KEEP ON AS WELL.

OH, SURE. IT'S REALLY CLOSE BY.

GO HALF A BLOCK DOWN THAT WAY, AND TAKE A RIGHT...

CHAPTER FIVE

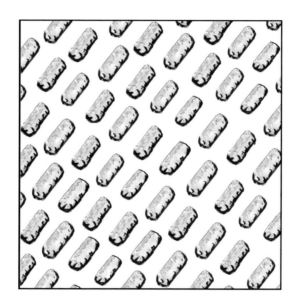

BURRITO
MATH

JULY
2017

IT WAS THE WORST
OF TIMES FOR OUR
NONPROFIT.

THE CITY'S COST OF LIVING WAS SKYROCKETING.

TO JUSTIFY OUR OFFICE'S RENT HIKE, OUR LANDLORD PITTED US AGAINST A SPECIALTY CHOCOLATIER AS WE TRIED TO RENEW OUR LEASE.

OUR NONPROFIT HAD SOME SUCCESS IN PASSING POLICIES TO INCREASE SOLAR ENERGY ACROSS CALIFORNIA, AND OUR JOB TRAINING CLASSES NOW HAD GRADUATES REGULARLY ENTERING INTO HIGH-WAGE CAREERS IN CONSTRUCTION.

BUT THE VALUE OF THE NONPROFIT'S WORK WASN'T UNDERSTOOD, AND WITH RAPID CHANGES HAPPENING ACROSS THE CITY, WE WERE LARGELY *INVISIBLE.*

SIGNAGE WASN'T MAKING US STAND OUT THAT MUCH MORE AT OUR OFFICE LOCATION ON HOWARD AND 6TH STREET.

PEOPLE PASSING BY WOULD LOOK AT THE WINDOW SIGNS AND ASK:

WHAT'S BRIGHTLINE?

I BEGAN TO PLAN AN EVENT THAT WOULD ACTIVATE OUR OFFICE, IN THE FORM OF AN OPEN HOUSE.

ONE OF BRIGHTLINE'S FIRST VOLUNTEERS, AASTHA, HAD SCAVENGED AN OLD WHITEBOARD.

AND A STAFF MEMBER BROUGHT PLANTS TO LIVEN UP THE OFFICE.

AASTHA FLOATED SOME IDEAS ON WHAT TO WRITE ON THE BOARD.

WE COULD DRAW THE LAYOUT OF OUR OFFICE...

...OR THE BOARD COULD DESCRIBE THE EVENT ITSELF!

IT'LL BE FOR WHEN PEOPLE ASK, "WHAT'S ON THE MENU?"

JUSTICE.

heh.

I FOUND THIS *HILARIOUS* IN A BLEAK WAY THAT OTHERS MIGHT NOT.

heh heh heh heh heh heh.

MOST PEOPLE DIDN'T KNOW THE COSTS AND LACK OF RESOURCES FOR OUR ENVIRONMENTAL JUSTICE WORK, AND EVEN FEWER KNEW OF THE FINANCIAL IMPACTS TO MY PERSONAL LIFE.

TO SURVIVE ON MY OWN MEAGER SALARY, I TURNED TO SIMPLER MATH.

FOR $7.99, A BURRITO CAME WITH ANY MEAT, RICE, BEANS, ONIONS, CILANTRO, SALSA.

FOR A DOLLAR EXTRA, YOU GOT CHEESE, SOUR CREAM, AVOCADO.

EVERYTHING INCLUDED, A BAY AREA BURRITO COULD REPLACE *TWO* MEALS.

ONCE I STARTED EATING FIVE A WEEK, I STARTED MEASURING *EVERYTHING* IN BURRITOS.

ONE WAS THE SAME COST AS A MARKER.

FOUR OR FIVE EQUALED A TANK OF GAS.

I LOST COUNT THINKING HOW MANY EQUALED MY LOANS FOR LAW SCHOOL.

BUT OTHERWISE, BURRITO MATH WAS SIMPLE.

$

OTHER MATH WAS NOT SO SIMPLE.

DING!

AH, YET ANOTHER REJECTION EMAIL.

OUR STAFF SPENT HUNDREDS OF HOURS WRITING GRANT PROPOSALS THAT DIDN'T CREATE MUCH RETURN.

brightline

WITH OUR OFFICE COSTS RISING, WE WERE RUNNING OUT OF TIME.

WE SEEMED TO FACE A CHICKEN-OR-THE-EGG DILEMMA: WITHOUT VISIBILITY, IT WAS TOUGH FOR OUR NONPROFIT TO GET FUNDING, AND TO BECOME VISIBLE, WE NEEDED MORE FUNDING.

FUNDRAISING FOR OUR NONPROFIT WAS AN UPHILL BATTLE, SO WE'D START WITH WHAT WE KNEW BEST:

BUILDING COMMUNITY.

I REMEMBER ANNY'S RESPONSE TO THESE STAKES.

...IF I HAD YOUR JOB, I WOULD HAVE HAD SEVERAL HEART ATTACKS BY NOW.

BUT AGAIN, THERE REALLY WASN'T TIME TO WORRY ABOUT HEART ATTACKS.

IF TIME ALLOWED, THE SIMPLEST AND MOST DIRECT APPROACH MADE FOR BETTER ORGANIZING.

FOR INSTANCE, A PHONE CALL WAS USUALLY MORE EFFECTIVE THAN EMAIL.

BUT A DIRECT ASK VIA PHONE TOOK TIME.

HEY, CAN YOU MAKE AN EVENT?

THURSDAY, THE 10TH...

...*YEP*, HOWARD 'N' 6TH STREET...

STARTS AT 5, LASTS UNTIL 7.

OUR NONPROFIT WORKED WITH DIVERSE LOCAL COMMUNITIES ON ISSUES RANGING FROM THE ENVIRONMENT TO EDUCATION.

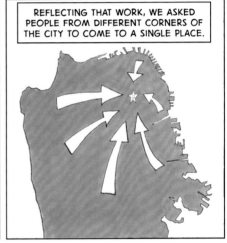

REFLECTING THAT WORK, WE ASKED PEOPLE FROM DIFFERENT CORNERS OF THE CITY TO COME TO A SINGLE PLACE.

GIVEN OUR LIMITED RESOURCES, WE COULDN'T SEND ALONG HAND-ENGRAVED INVITATIONS.

SO ROUND-THE-CLOCK COMMUNICATION AND *PATIENCE* WERE KEY.

NO, NOT AUGUST 17TH...THE *10TH*. SO *NEXT* WEEK.

Luminalt

Solar for Your Home & Business 415.641.4000

SUNFLOWER

JUST BEFORE AN EVENT, MASS EMAILS WERE GOOD FOR VISIBILITY.

PERSONALLY, I HATED THEM.

DE-DUPING CONTACTS IS THE WORST--

HELLO.

THE LISTS ARE DE-DUPLICATED. JUST CLICK REFRESH.

OH, OK. THANKS, CLAIRE.

VOLUNTEERS LIKE CLAIRE HELPED IN FIXING OUR GAPS IN EMAIL AND SOCIAL MEDIA.

STILL, AUTHENTIC COMMUNICATION ONLINE WAS TOUGH.

OVER THE YEARS, WE SLOWLY BUILT OUT MANY DIFFERENT TOOLS TO PROMOTE THE EVENT...

Brightline Ope
Francisco, C

mailchimp

JULY 2019

WHICH IS WHY ART WAS ALSO KEY TO PROMOTING OUR OPEN HOUSE.

WITH DONATED ART FROM ME.

THE PRINTS WERE PRIZES IN A GAME.

IF YOU TOSS A BALL IN THE CUP, YOU CAN WIN THIS ART PRINT!

CUTE. WHO DREW THIS?

PROMOTING THE ART AS MINE DIDN'T MATTER MUCH.

AS LONG AS PEOPLE ENJOYED THEMSELVES.

♪ Ta-da! ♪

IN 2017, OUR OPEN HOUSE WAS PLANNED AS A SMALLER GATHERING.

Welcome

NICE! I LIKE IT.

AND OVER THE YEARS, FRIENDS NOTICED THE EVENT'S GROWTH.

DANG, GOT A LOT OF PEOPLE THIS YEAR.

YEAH, TOOK SOME DOING.

IT'S NATURAL TO KEEP BUILDING ON INITIAL SUCCESS...

...BUT LOSING QUALITY FOR QUANTITY WAS NEVER AN OPTION.

STORIES WERE *BETTER* WHEN SHARED WITH PEOPLE WHO WERE THERE FROM THE BEGINNING.

REMEMBER THE EARLY DAYS, KENNETH?

OH YEAH, WE SORTED BOXES OF PAPER FOR WEEKS.

THERE WAS A BIG COMMUNAL TABLE *COVERED* IN OLD FORMS AND REPORTS.

"...YEP, A TABLE BURIED IN PAPER A FOOT HIGH."

HELP!

YEAH, I REMEMBER THAT TABLE.

THE MESS STRETCHED FROM ONE END OF THIS ROOM TO THE OTHER...

OF COURSE, EVERY STORY HAS AN ENDING.

...WOW, TIME REALLY FLEW.

I THOUGHT THAT WAS GOOD, EDDIE.

IF YOU DON'T NEED ANYTHING ELSE, I'M TAKING OFF!

A LOT OF PEOPLE TOOK TIME OUT OF THEIR DAY TO COME.

THANKS, AASTHA!

UMMA, PLEASE TAKE OFF...I HAVE TO CLEAN UP JUST A BIT MORE.

THERE WAS ALWAYS ENOUGH WORK TO BE HERE ALL NIGHT LONG...

BUT I HAVE TO REMIND MYSELF THAT THIS WORK IS MORE ABOUT ENDURANCE, RATHER THAN A SPRINT TO A SINGLE VICTORY.

VRRRRRRRRRMM

LEAVING WORK WOULD BE ALRIGHT FOR NOW...

...AS OUR DOORS WOULD BE OPEN FOR MORE THE NEXT DAY.

THANKS TO EACH OPEN HOUSE, WE ACCUMULATED *JUST ENOUGH* SMALL DONATIONS TO SURVIVE A FEW MORE MONTHS.

BY GROWING OUR OPEN HOUSE EVENT OVER THE YEARS, WE EXPANDED OUR CONNECTIONS AND EVENTUALLY APPLIED FOR NEW GRANTS IN AIR QUALITY AND WIND ENERGY RESEARCH.

THE QUIET AFTER THIS EVENT NEVER LASTED FOR LONG THOUGH.

AS I TRIED TO RELAX OVER DRINKS WITH GUILLERMO, HE TOSSED OUT A NEW IDEA...

129

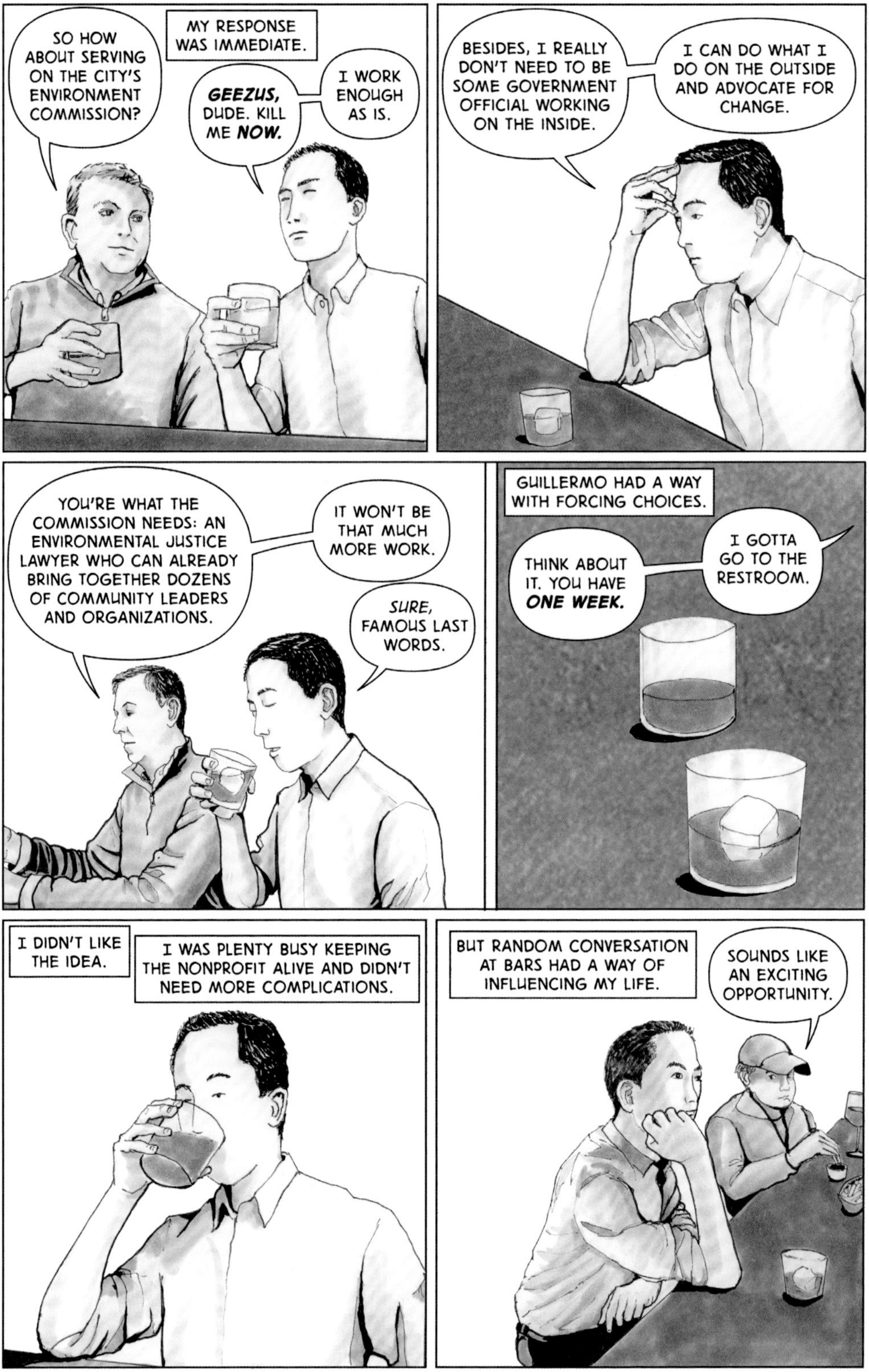
SO HOW ABOUT SERVING ON THE CITY'S ENVIRONMENT COMMISSION?
MY RESPONSE WAS IMMEDIATE.
GEEZUS, DUDE. KILL ME **NOW.**
I WORK ENOUGH AS IS.
BESIDES, I REALLY DON'T NEED TO BE SOME GOVERNMENT OFFICIAL WORKING ON THE INSIDE.
I CAN DO WHAT I DO ON THE OUTSIDE AND ADVOCATE FOR CHANGE.
YOU'RE WHAT THE COMMISSION NEEDS: AN ENVIRONMENTAL JUSTICE LAWYER WHO CAN ALREADY BRING TOGETHER DOZENS OF COMMUNITY LEADERS AND ORGANIZATIONS.
IT WON'T BE THAT MUCH MORE WORK.
SURE, FAMOUS LAST WORDS.
GUILLERMO HAD A WAY WITH FORCING CHOICES.
THINK ABOUT IT. YOU HAVE **ONE WEEK.**
I GOTTA GO TO THE RESTROOM.
I DIDN'T LIKE THE IDEA.
I WAS PLENTY BUSY KEEPING THE NONPROFIT ALIVE AND DIDN'T NEED MORE COMPLICATIONS.
BUT RANDOM CONVERSATION AT BARS HAD A WAY OF INFLUENCING MY LIFE.
SOUNDS LIKE AN EXCITING OPPORTUNITY.

OH, IT'S NOT THAT EXCITING.

I WAS GRUMPIER THAN I SHOULD HAVE BEEN.

RIGHT NOW, I WORK AT AN ENVIRONMENTAL POLICY NONPROFIT, AND A GOVERNMENT AGENCY WOULD BE USING MY EXPERIENCE.

SURE, BEING A COMMISSIONER IS A LEADERSHIP ROLE, BUT IT'S NOT A FULL-TIME JOB. JUST A WHOLE LOTTA EXTRA WORK.

SO WHAT WOULD YOU GET TO DO?

THIS WOULD BE ABOUT SERVING ON A COMMISSION THAT SETS POLICY FOR THE ENVIRONMENT DEPARTMENT.

CITY & COUNTY OF SAN FRANCISCO

Commission on the Environment

THE ENVIRONMENT DEPARTMENT HAS ABOUT 100 STAFFERS WORKING ON LEGISLATION AND PUBLIC OUTREACH, AS WELL AS COLLABORATING WITH OTHER LOCAL, STATE, AND FEDERAL AGENCIES.

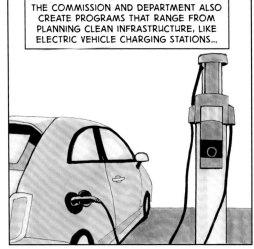

THE COMMISSION AND DEPARTMENT ALSO CREATE PROGRAMS THAT RANGE FROM PLANNING CLEAN INFRASTRUCTURE, LIKE ELECTRIC VEHICLE CHARGING STATIONS...

LANDFILL COMPOST RECYCLE

...TO WASTE MANAGEMENT, RECYCLING, AND MORE.

WHILE WORKING THROUGH MORE FRIES AND RED WINE, THE STRANGER THOUGHT ABOUT ALL THIS FOR A BEAT, BEFORE DECLARING:

SOUNDS LIKE COOL WORK.

IT'S NICE TO GET ASKED TO DO STUFF.

I DIDN'T HAVE A QUICK RESPONSE TO THIS.

...

WITH MORE STAFF AND FOCUSED PROGRAMS, AN ENVIRONMENTAL COMMISSIONER COULD HAVE GREATER IMPACT AND GRAPPLE WITH LARGER PROBLEMS IN CLIMATE CHANGE.

WHILE I WOULD EVENTUALLY TAKE ON THE ENVIRONMENTAL COMMISSIONER POSITION, MY LIFE BALANCE WAS NOT JUST ABOUT BEING A COMMISSIONER AND RUNNING A NONPROFIT...

...BUT ALSO CREATING ART.

WORKING OFF AN OLD DRAWING DESK DONATED FROM A FRIEND, I HAD SPENT **HUNDREDS** OF HOURS IMPROVING MY LINEWORK AND COLORING.

I ALSO SLOWLY TAUGHT MYSELF ASPECTS OF GRAPHIC DESIGN AND DIGITAL EDITING AFTER SCANNING IN MY HAND-DRAWN ILLUSTRATIONS.

AS A RESULT, MY ART EVOLVED RAPIDLY.

I COULD NOW ILLUSTRATE BUSINESSES AND INSTITUTIONS RECOGNIZABLE TO LOCALS...

AS WELL AS LANDMARKS KNOWN TO THE WORLD.

AND AMID ALL THIS WORK, I RELIED ON ANNY FOR ADVICE.

WHAT DO YOU THINK?

SHE HAD BEEN IN DIFFERENT LINES OF WORK HERSELF IN ARCHITECTURE AND NURSING. AFTER BEING FRIENDS FOR YEARS, WE HAD BECOME CLOSER.

HEE HEE... MAYBE ADD COLOR TO THE BIRD?

YEP, THINKING ABOUT TWO OR THREE SHADES!

...YOU ALSO SMELL GOOD TODAY!

JUST TODAY?

ANNY UNDERSTOOD AND ADAPTED TO ALL THESE PROJECTS...

...SO THAT THE BALANCE BETWEEN MY PERSONAL LIFE AND WORK BECAME MORE SETTLED.

133

WITH MY IMPROVED DRAWING SKILLS, I FELT CONFIDENT ABOUT PURSUING NEW OPPORTUNITIES.

THERE WAS A COMPETITION TO INSTALL ART ON METAL UTILITY BOXES, WHICH WERE LOCATED ON SIDEWALKS THROUGHOUT THE CITY. THESE BOXES HOUSED EQUIPMENT FOR HIGH-SPEED INTERNET AND COMMUNICATION SERVICES.

MY ART WAS CHOSEN AND PRINTED ON WEATHER-RESILIENT WRAPS, WHICH WERE THEN BLOWTORCHED ONTO 10 OF THESE BOXES.

THIS ART WAS FOR THE COMMUNITY, AND MY NEIGHBORS APPRECIATED ITS DETAILS.

HOWEVER, I WASN'T SURE HOW MY FAMILY WOULD REACT. MY FATHER WAS ESPECIALLY HARD TO REACH AFTER HE MOVED OUT OF OUR FAMILY HOME IN TEXAS...

...SO I INVITED MY DAD TO VISIT SAN FRANCISCO AND TAKE A LOOK.

HE STILL DIDN'T SEEM TO CARE ABOUT MY NONPROFIT CAREER OR COMICS WORK, SO MY EXPECTATIONS WERE LOW.

〈HUH, IT'S A TOFU SOUP RESTAURANT.〉

BUT TO MY SURPRISE, HE REALLY ENJOYED THESE ART INSTALLATIONS.

HE TOOK PICTURES OF EACH BOX...

...AND EVEN LEANED AGAINST THEM, AS IF HE WAS TESTING WHETHER THEY WERE REAL.

BUT THERE WERE OTHER REMINDERS OF HOW MY DAD COULD BE DIFFICULT.

<YOU CAN PARK IN MY GARAGE, AND WE'LL PICK YOU UP.>

WHILE HE WAS IN SAN FRANCISCO, ANNY AND I TRIED TO MAKE HIS STAY COMFORTABLE.

THE GARAGE CODE IS 5-9-2-3.

OK, 5-2-3-9?

<NO, IT'S 5-9-2-3.>

HEHEHE!

IT'S NOT WORKING. 5-3-2...

NO.

WHETHER IN ENGLISH OR IN KOREAN, LISTENING WAS NEVER MY DAD'S STRONG SUIT.

...7-5...

NO!

I HAD TO REMIND MYSELF TO BE PATIENT.

NO, LISTEN CAREFULLY...

HE RARELY BOTHERED REMEMBERING DETAILS LIKE BIRTHDAYS AND OTHER PEOPLE'S NAMES.

HIS INABILITY TO REPEAT BACK A FOUR-DIGIT CODE SIGNALED GREATER TURMOIL AHEAD.

IN 2019, I DIDN'T KNOW THE SEVERITY OF HIS SITUATION, BUT MY DAD'S LIFE HAD BEEN UNRAVELING OVER THE YEARS.

DECLARING HE WAS BORED AND WANTED TO SEE MORE OF MY LIFE, HE CHOSE TO STAY AT A MOTEL NEAR MY APARTMENT.

BUT HE REVERTED TO HIS USUAL MERCURIAL SELF...

WHATCHA DOING, APPA?

...BY SUDDENLY DECIDING HE WOULD MOVE BACK TO SEOUL WITH HIS REMAINING ITEMS.

〈HELP ME ORGANIZE, EDDIE.〉

SOME CLOTHING, PAPERS, GOLF CLUBS...

...A PLAQUE CELEBRATING THE COMPLETION OF HIS MASTER'S DEGREE IN THE UNITED STATES...

CONGRATULATIONS ON YOUR GRADUATION
DUCK YONG AHN, M.S
WE ALL WISH YOU A HAPPY AND BRIGHT FUTURE
FROM ALUMNI OF SEOUL HIGH
AT THE UNIVERSITY OF TEXAS AUSTIN MARCH 1984

...AND PERHAPS MOST SURPRISINGLY, ONE OF MY OLD COMIC BOOKS MADE YEARS AGO.

I DIDN'T KNOW HE CARED ABOUT MY COMICS AT ALL.

MY DAD MIGHT HAVE ALSO APPRECIATED THE **WORK ETHIC** BEHIND GROWING THE NONPROFIT AS A SMALL BUSINESS.

TK TK TK TK

AS WILDFIRES RAGED IN 2018 AND 2019...

...DANIELA AND I DEDICATED MANY MORE MONTHS TO RESEARCH AND WRITE A GRANT APPLICATION FOR AIR QUALITY MONITORING.

OUR GRANTS OFTEN FUNDED LARGER PARTNERSHIPS...

...SUCH AS OTHER NONPROFITS, ACADEMIC RESEARCHERS, ENVIRONMENTAL TECH START-UPS, AND GOVERNMENT AGENCIES.

...HOW ABOUT PAGE 48?

I THINK IT'S REALLY CLOSE.

ULTIMATELY, THE RESPONSIBILITY WOULD BE WITH OUR NONPROFIT TO DELIVER THIS STATE GRANT BEFORE THE SUBMISSION DEADLINE.

Sacramento   Fair[

EMAIL SUBMISSION WAS NOT ALLOWED IN 2019, SO I PERSONALLY DROVE TO THE STATE CAPITOL AND HAND-DELIVERED IT.

ON THE WAY BACK, I REALIZED I HADN'T EATEN ALL DAY AGAIN.

ALRIGHT, STOMACH. YOU WILL BE FED.

GROWL

L8WRRI

AND I RETURNED TO MY FAVORITE RESTAURANT FROM MY EARLIER NONPROFIT DAYS IN OAKLAND.

BACK AGAIN, BACK AGAIN...

...BACK TO THE SCENE OF THE CRIME.

SIGN'S SHOWING ITS AGE, BUT THIS PLACE WAS ABOUT THE SAME AS I REMEMBERED.

FOOD WAS THE SAME TOO, MORE OR LESS:

HAND-PULLED NOODLES.

DRY-BRAISED GREEN BEANS.

BACK IN THE DAY, I'D GET THE SAME DISH.

ONE ORDER OF SHAN DONG DUMPLINGS, PLEASE.

EVEN THE SAME FAMILY WORKED THE COUNTER AND TABLES.

THEY'VE BEEN HERE FOR ALMOST 30 YEARS.

THE OWNER, CHARLES, USUALLY HAS A READY QUIP.

SURPRISINGLY, HE RECOGNIZED ME EVEN THOUGH I HAVEN'T STOPPED BY IN A LONG WHILE.

BACK THEN, YOU LOOK LIKE A *BOY*. NOW YOU LOOK A LITTLE MORE LIKE A *MAN*.

HEH!

YEP, SAME OL' CHARLES.

I THOUGHT BACK TO MY FIRST EXPERIENCE HERE IN 2005.

HAVING FINISHED A LONG DAY WITH THE YOUTH, I NEEDED TO REFUEL.

WHILE BURRITOS WERE MORE FILLING, I LIKED HOW THE LITTLE THINGS IN THIS RESTAURANT REMINDED ME OF MY FAMILY'S LIQUOR STORE.

THE BACKGROUND CHATTER WITH CUSTOMERS OVER THE COUNTER...

...THE QUICK MOVEMENTS OF CHARLES AS HE RUSHED FROM CUSTOMER TO CUSTOMER...

...AND THE DEDICATED LABOR IN SOMETHING SO SEEMINGLY SIMPLE.

I TOOK MY DUMPLINGS TO GO, AS I WANTED TO SEE HOW THE NEIGHBORHOOD HAD DEVELOPED.

I KEPT WALKING DOWN 10TH STREET, LOOKING FOR A QUIET SPOT TO EAT.

THE ELEMENTARY SCHOOL WHERE I HAD WORKED WAS A BLOCK AWAY.

I HALF-EXPECTED SOMEONE TO YELL *"EDDIE GUERRERO!"* FROM THE PLAYGROUND.

BUT OF COURSE, ALL THE STUDENTS I WORKED WITH WERE LONG GONE.

I WONDERED IF THEY WOULD HAVE UNDERSTOOD MY ENVIRONMENTAL JUSTICE CAREER.

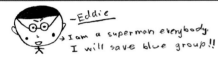

THE YOUTH APPRECIATED MY SERVICE TO THEM, BUT EVEN IN THEIR PLAYFUL NOTES, I WORRIED THEY SAW ME AS SOME SORT OF HERO...

...WHEN I NEVER MUCH BELIEVED IN HERO-DRIVEN NARRATIVES.

NO ONE THAT I'VE WORKED WITH NEEDS TO BE *"SAVED."*

COMMUNITIES ARE RESILIENT AND CAN TAKE CARE OF THEMSELVES, WHETHER I'M AROUND OR NOT.

RATHER, IT'S ABOUT LENDING SKILLS AND BEING GENEROUS. THE GOALS WERE THE *SAME* WHETHER WORKING WITH *MAMA JACKSON* OR RUNNING A JOB TRAINING PROGRAM:

EMPOWERED COMMUNITIES, *SUSTAINABLE* ENVIRONMENTS.

THAT'S WHY I'VE ALSO BEEN OK WITH REMINDERS OF HOW MY TIME AND WORK WITH COMMUNITIES MAY BE FLEETING.

HEY, *EDDIE GUERRERO.* YOU *DIED* TODAY.

I'VE TAKEN JOY IN THE SMALL DETAILS ALONG THE WAY.

THESE DUMPLINGS, FOR EXAMPLE.

MADE IN A SMALL, UNCHANGED CORNER OF THE WORLD.

HERE'S TO HOPING A LOT OF WORK CAN LEAD TO SOMETHING WORTHWHILE.

BECAUSE 15 YEARS LATER, I'M STILL A NONPROFIT WORKER EATING DUMPLINGS.

Munch! Munch! Munch!

TASTES AS GOOD AS EVER.

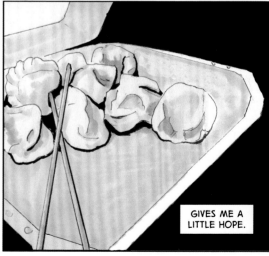

GIVES ME A LITTLE HOPE.

CHAPTER SIX

FRONTLINES

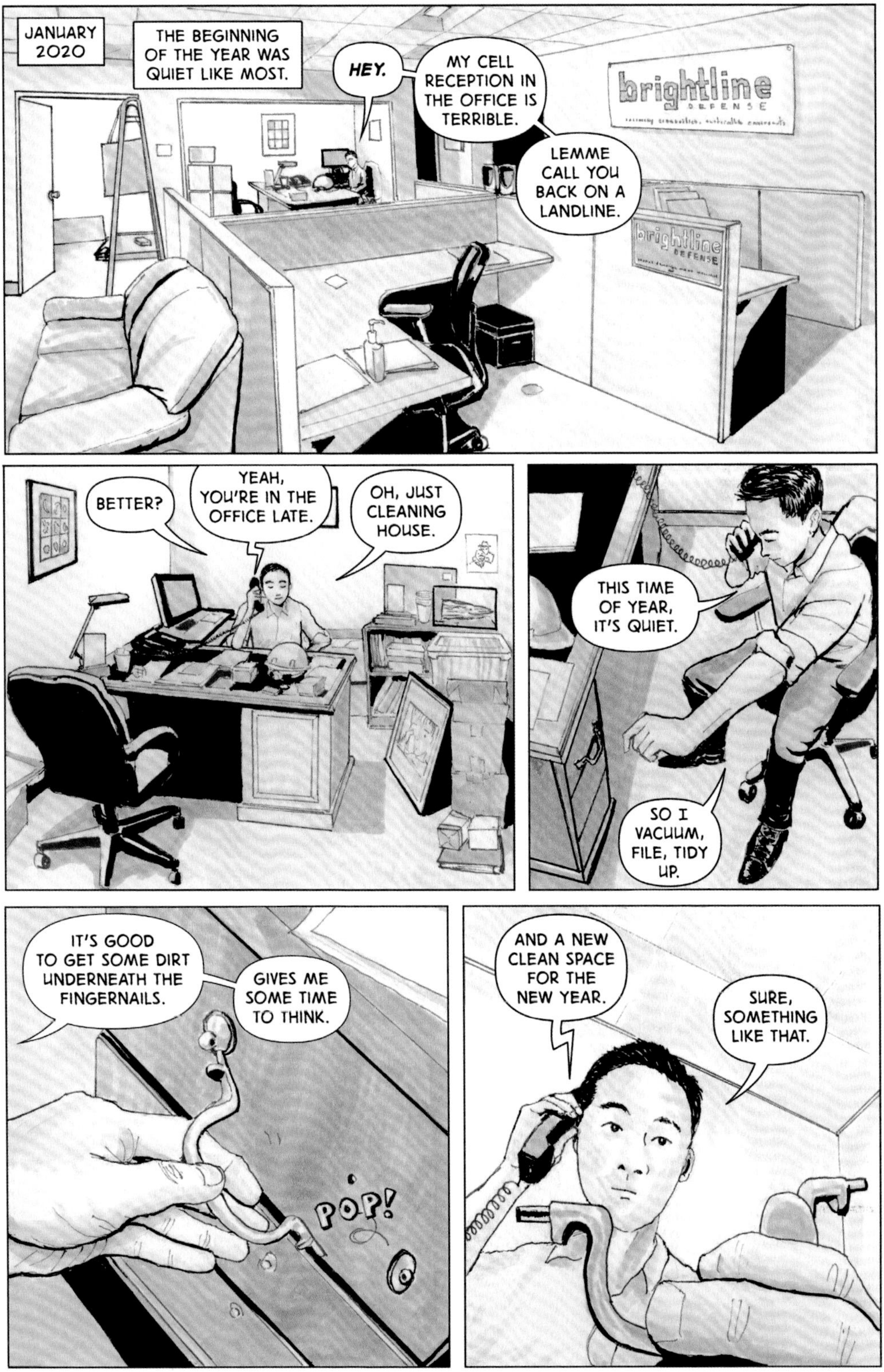
JANUARY 2020
THE BEGINNING OF THE YEAR WAS QUIET LIKE MOST.
HEY.
MY CELL RECEPTION IN THE OFFICE IS TERRIBLE.
LEMME CALL YOU BACK ON A LANDLINE.
brightline DEFENSE
BETTER?
YEAH, YOU'RE IN THE OFFICE LATE.
OH, JUST CLEANING HOUSE.
THIS TIME OF YEAR, IT'S QUIET.
SO I VACUUM, FILE, TIDY UP.
IT'S GOOD TO GET SOME DIRT UNDERNEATH THE FINGERNAILS.
GIVES ME SOME TIME TO THINK.
POP!
AND A NEW CLEAN SPACE FOR THE NEW YEAR.
SURE, SOMETHING LIKE THAT.

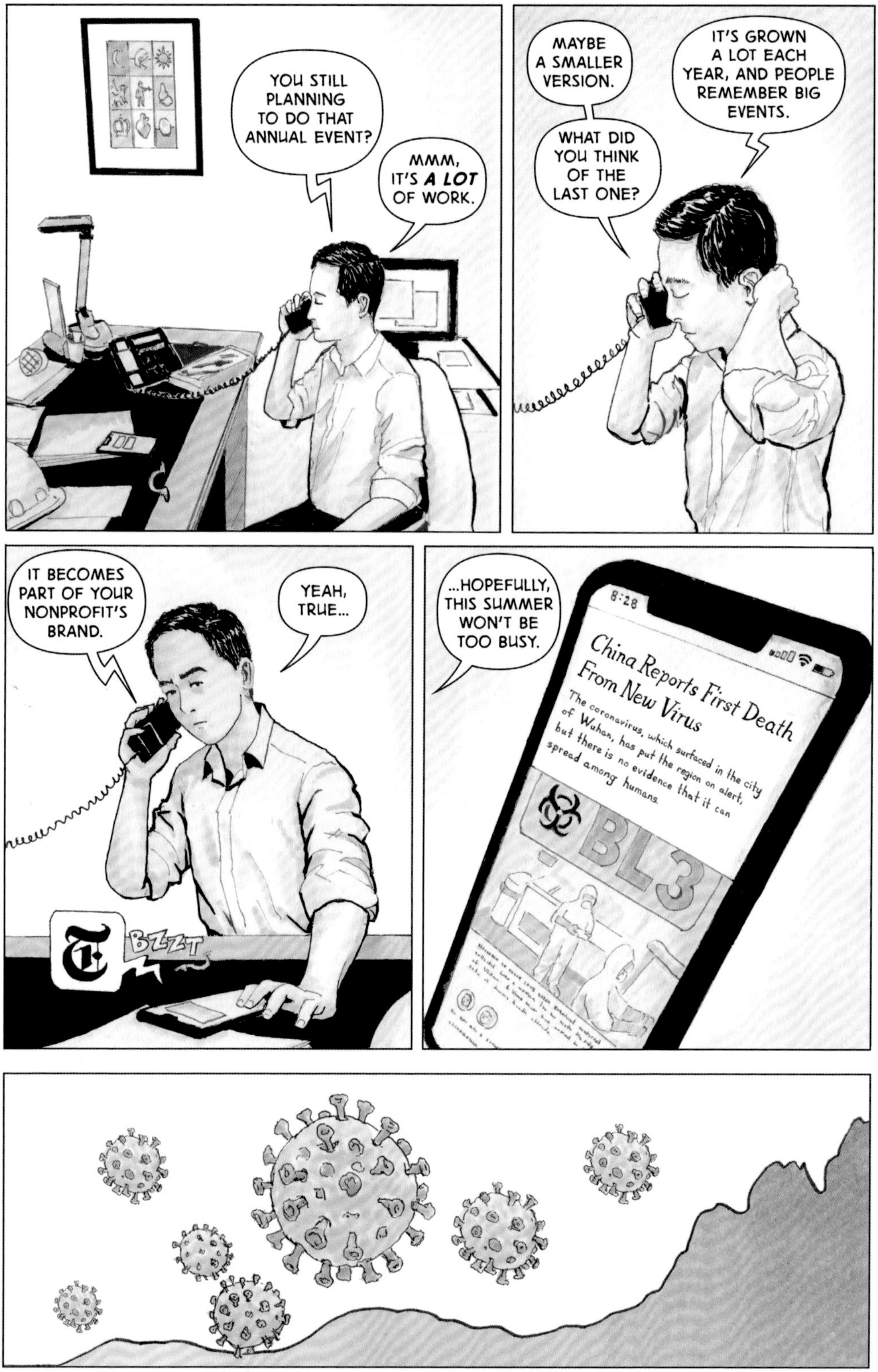
YOU STILL PLANNING TO DO THAT ANNUAL EVENT?
MMM, IT'S **A LOT** OF WORK.
MAYBE A SMALLER VERSION.
WHAT DID YOU THINK OF THE LAST ONE?
IT'S GROWN A LOT EACH YEAR, AND PEOPLE REMEMBER BIG EVENTS.
IT BECOMES PART OF YOUR NONPROFIT'S BRAND.
YEAH, TRUE...
BZZT
...HOPEFULLY, THIS SUMMER WON'T BE TOO BUSY.
8:28
China Reports First Death From New Virus
The coronavirus, which surfaced in the city of Wuhan, has put the region on alert, but there is no evidence that it can spread among humans.
BL3

WE OFTEN PURCHASED SUPPLIES IN BULK TO SAVE ON COSTS FOR OUR PROGRAMMING.

THESE SNACKS WEREN'T EXCITING, BUT THERE WAS LIMITED FUNDING FOR OUR NONPROFIT'S JOB TRAINING AND YOUTH PROGRAMS.

EACH PURCHASE WAS WEIGHED CAREFULLY AMONG ALL THE CHOICES.

CONTRAST THIS WITH THE EARLY DAYS OF 2020.

MARCH 2020

WHEN SHELVES WERE CLEARED AND SCARCITY AMPED UP THE ANXIETY.

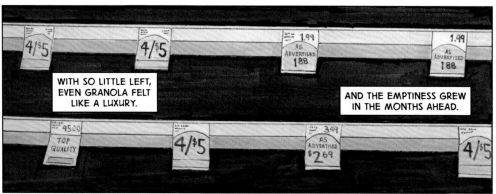

WITH SO LITTLE LEFT, EVEN GRANOLA FELT LIKE A LUXURY.

AND THE EMPTINESS GREW IN THE MONTHS AHEAD.

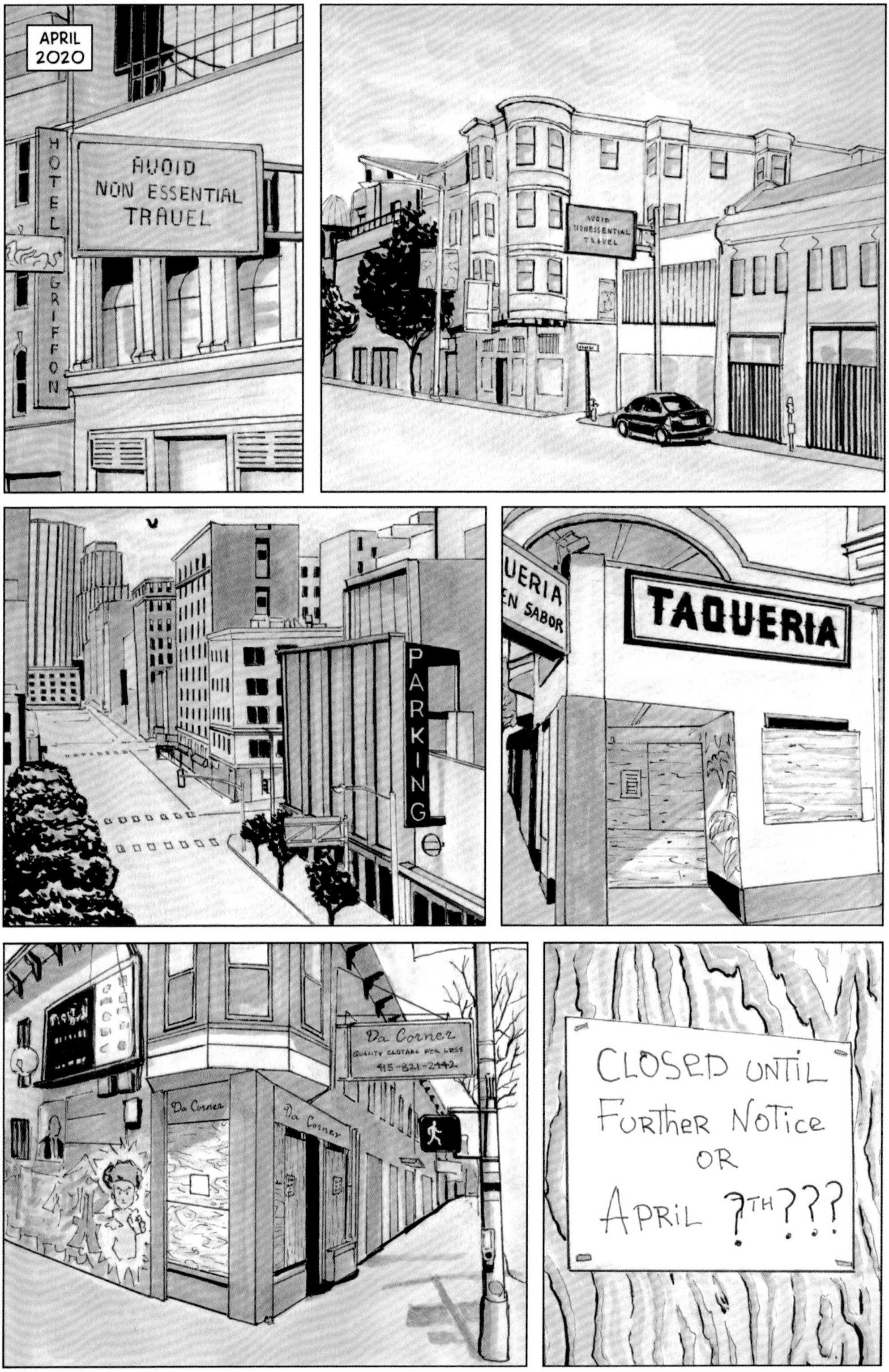
APRIL 2020
HOTEL GRIFFON
AVOID NON ESSENTIAL TRAVEL
AVOID NONESSENTIAL TRAVEL
PARKING
TAQUERIA
Da Corner
Quality Clothes for Less
415-821-2442
Da Corner
Da Corner
CLOSED UNTIL
FURTHER NOTICE
OR
APRIL 7TH???

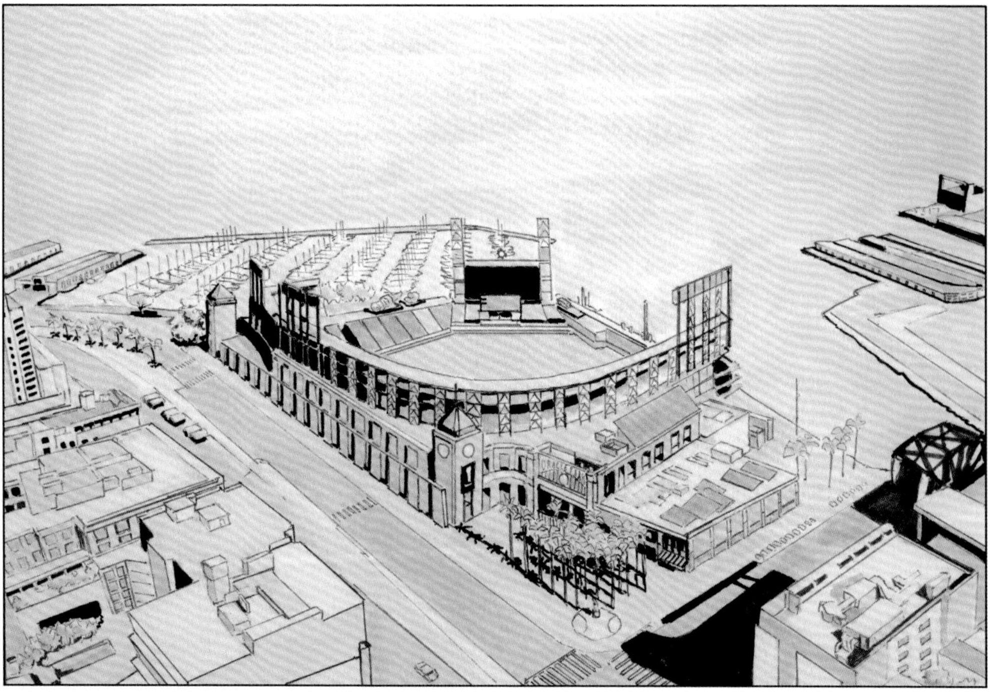

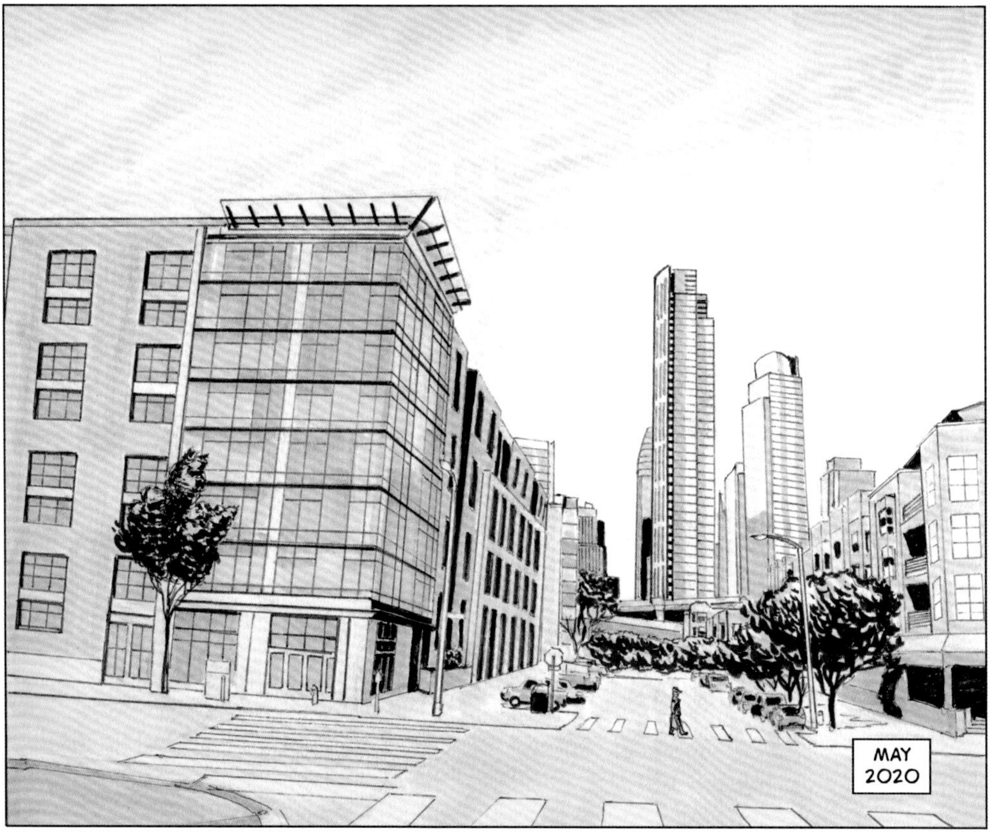
MAY
2020

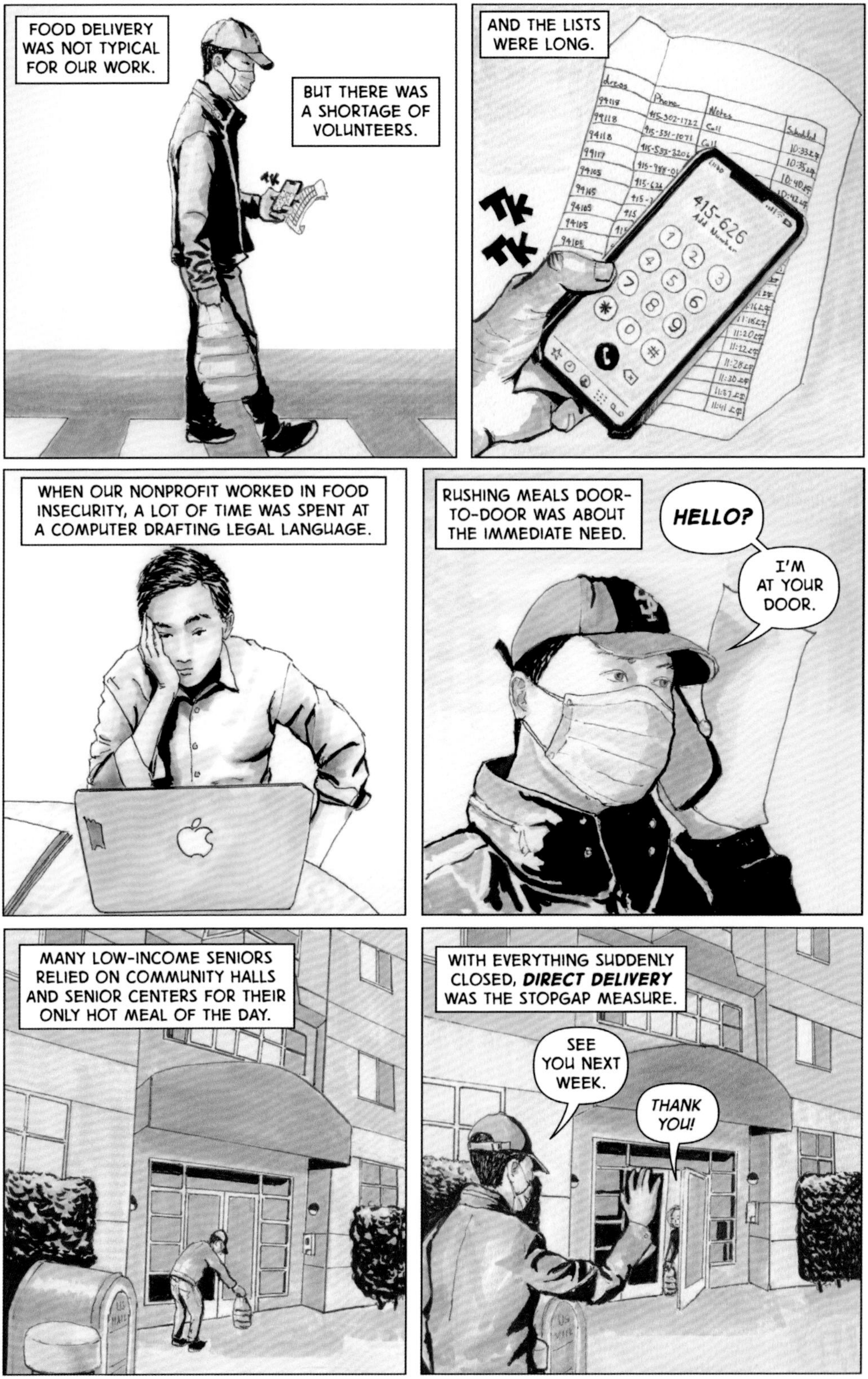
FOOD DELIVERY WAS NOT TYPICAL FOR OUR WORK.
BUT THERE WAS A SHORTAGE OF VOLUNTEERS.
AND THE LISTS WERE LONG.
TK
TK
415-626
WHEN OUR NONPROFIT WORKED IN FOOD INSECURITY, A LOT OF TIME WAS SPENT AT A COMPUTER DRAFTING LEGAL LANGUAGE.
RUSHING MEALS DOOR-TO-DOOR WAS ABOUT THE IMMEDIATE NEED.
HELLO?
I'M AT YOUR DOOR.
MANY LOW-INCOME SENIORS RELIED ON COMMUNITY HALLS AND SENIOR CENTERS FOR THEIR ONLY HOT MEAL OF THE DAY.
WITH EVERYTHING SUDDENLY CLOSED, DIRECT DELIVERY WAS THE STOPGAP MEASURE.
SEE YOU NEXT WEEK.
THANK YOU!

SENIOR CENTER KITCHENS BECAME PACKING HUBS FOR THE MEALS AS WELL AS PLANNING CENTERS FOR DELIVERY ROUTES AND ESSENTIAL WORKERS.

HEY, MAN.

I HELP LOAD THE CAR.

SERVING FAMILIES IN LARGE RESIDENTIAL BUILDINGS WAS A UNIQUE CHALLENGE.

WHERE YOU GOING TODAY?

ST. CLAIRE.

OK, GOOD LUCK, MAN.

CROWDING WAS AN ISSUE IN THE EARLIER DAYS.

AFTER RUNNING OUT OF MEALS, I WOULD RETURN TO THE KITCHENS FOR MORE AND CIRCLE BACK.

PAYING ATTENTION TO SMALL DETAILS AND ESTABLISHING ROUTINES HELPED MINIMIZE RISK AND INEFFICIENCIES.

TO TRANSPORT SEVERAL LARGE BOXES, I WOULD USE MY OWN CAR AND THE QUICKEST STREETS.

I ALSO MEMORIZED THE BEST PARKING SPOTS FOR EASIER UNLOADING.

THESE METHODS HELPED IN SERVING SINGLE-ROOM OCCUPANCY HOTELS (SROs), A TYPE OF DENSE HOUSING FOR LOW-INCOME TENANTS.

SROS WERE OLDER BUILDINGS, OFTEN BUILT OVER A CENTURY AGO.

ELEVATOR ACCESS WAS LIMITED, SO I TOOK THE STAIRS.

SRO ROOMS WERE SMALL, TYPICALLY 8 BY 10 FEET.

POSSESSIONS SOMETIMES PILED UP AGAINST THE WALLS AND HUNG FROM THE CEILING.

KITCHENS, TOILETS, AND SHOWERS WERE DOWN THE HALLWAY, SHARED AMONG RESIDENTS.

OUTBREAKS COULD EASILY HAPPEN IN THESE CLOSE LIVING QUARTERS.

NOT SURPRISINGLY, SRO MEAL DELIVERY WAS SOLITARY WORK.

EVEN WITH ENTIRE FAMILIES LIVING IN ONE ROOM, I RARELY TALKED TO ANYONE.

WHILE STOPPING BY EACH HOME, I THOUGHT ABOUT THE DISPROPORTIONATE RISK IN FRONTLINE COMMUNITIES.

AND HOW INADEQUATE MY WORK FELT.

WITH EVERYTHING ELSE SHUT DOWN, NONPROFITS RAMPED UP THEIR SERVICE.

JUNE 2020, CHINATOWN

VOLUNTEER LABOR WAS NEEDED TO GO INTO ALL CORNERS OF THE CITY...

MISSION DISTRICT

RICHMOND DISTRICT

SOUTH OF MARKET

OCEANVIEW

...AND THE WORKLOAD KEPT INCREASING OVER TIME.

ALL THIS MADE IT HARD TO SLOW DOWN, BUT EVENTUALLY, IT WAS A COMMUNITY ORGANIZER WHO REPRIMANDED ME.

YOU NEED TO TAKE CARE OF YOURSELF, MAN.

YOU'RE AN EXECUTIVE DIRECTOR TOO.

SHARE THE RISK WITH STAFF.

YEAH, YEAH.

THIS WAS HARD TO ACCEPT, AS I WAS ALREADY PLANNING THE NEXT DELIVERY.

OUR BEST WORK WAS OFTEN IN THE MINUTIAE OF PROGRAMS.

NO DETAIL WAS TOO SMALL, LIKE FIXING A SNACK SHORTAGE FOR JOB TRAINEES.

AND WHILE THIS HANDS-ON ATTENTION WASN'T FLASHY...

...THE RESULTS WERE TANGIBLE.

STILL, I HAD TO ACCEPT THE REALITY THAT I WASN'T A SUPERHERO.

I COULDN'T BE EVERYWHERE, ALL THE TIME.

THE ORGANIZER WAS RIGHT.

TAKING CARE OF ONESELF WAS IMPORTANT.

AFTER ALL, THE WORK WAS NEVER ABOUT MOMENTS OF SPECTACULAR COURAGE...

...BUT RATHER, A QUIET KIND OF GRIT TO CARRY ON, *DAY AFTER DAY*...

...THE BUILDING OF COMMUNITY THROUGH SIMPLE ROUTINES.

GOTCHYER GRANOLA BARS HERE!

AW, MAN.

GRANOLA BARS AGAIN?

YEP... AGAIN.

INSTEAD OF CONSTANTLY EATING ON THE GO, I TOOK BREAKS BY EATING BURRITOS ALONE IN MY OFFICE.

AS WITH THE BEGINNING OF PRIOR YEARS, I SAVORED THE QUIET WHILE PREPARING FOR FUTURE WORK.

JULY 2020

UNFORTUNATELY, BY COMING TO THE OFFICE, I ALSO BECAME AWARE OF OTHER RISKS.

oh!

chinese f#cker

!

PROPPING OPEN THE OFFICE DOOR WITH A BOX OF SUPPLIES, I STRUGGLED WITH HOW TO RESPOND.

DO I LET THIS GO?

CHASE DOWN AND CONFRONT THE PERSON?

DEMAND AN APOLOGY?

LARKIN

JUST A WEEK LATER, WHILE SURVEYING LOCATIONS IN THE TENDERLOIN FOR INSTALLING AIR QUALITY SENSORS:

QUOR

~grmph.

I'mma j@p slap you...

VISIBILITY OVER ANTI-ASIAN VIOLENCE WOULD PEAK IN 2021, BUT THESE TWO INCIDENTS BROUGHT ME BACK TO THE PAST...

...WITH EXPERIENCES THAT HAVEN'T BEEN LIMITED BY TIME OR GEOGRAPHY.

PROVIDENCE, RI, 2004

ching chong chang

HA HA HA HA

!

SCREECH!

I'VE LOST COUNT HOW MANY TIMES I'VE EXPERIENCED MOCK FOREIGN LANGUAGE TAUNTS.

BUT I DO REMEMBER NO RESPONSE EVER FELT ADEQUATE.

WHEN I WAS A GROCERY STORE CASHIER DURING COLLEGE, A CUSTOMER ONCE SNAPPED AT ME.

YOU SHOULD **GO BACK** TO WHERE YOU CAME FROM.

FROM YEARS OF WORKING A REGISTER, THE POLITE AND FIRM REJECTION CAME EASILY ENOUGH.

SORRY. WE DON'T SERVE RACISTS HERE.

STILL, HER DISMISSIVE TONE LINGERED AS SHE WALKED AWAY.

WHAT?! I'm a racist?!

FINE.

WOULD IT BE ANY DIFFERENT IN THE FUTURE?

IN 2020, THERE WASN'T MUCH TIME FOR SELF-REFLECTION.

BEGINNING IN AUGUST, WILDFIRES CONSUMED THE WEST COAST FOR MONTHS.

SEPTEMBER 2020

SMOKE FROM THE FIRES SETTLED OVER THE CITY, TURNING THE SKY AN APOCALYPTIC ORANGE.

NO STOPPING ANY TIME

LOW-INCOME COMMUNITIES DIDN'T HAVE SENSORS TO TRACK LOCAL AIR QUALITY IMPACTS, AND OUR NONPROFIT RUSHED TO FILL IN THE GAPS.

ROOFTOP ACCESS WASN'T EASY TO FIND, AS MOST OFFICES WERE CLOSED.

DANIELA AND I WORKED WITH OTHER NONPROFIT STAFF TO OPEN UP THEIR OFFICES AND ROOFTOPS FOR SENSOR INSTALLATION.

LADDER'S IN THE BACK, AND WE CLEARED OFF THE DESK.

THE HANDS-ON NATURE OF THE WORK LED TO MOMENTS NOT TYPICAL OF A DESK JOB...

...LIKE BEING PERCHED *ON* THE DESK, THINKING THROUGH THE NEXT STEP:

HOW TO WORK TOGETHER AND EMERGE FROM CRISIS.

A JOY OF THE WORK WAS THE UNEXPECTED CREATIVITY IN TAKING ON CHALLENGES...

...AS A TEAM... IN COMMUNITY.

GOMA
HOTEL
APARTMENTS
MODERN IN EVERY PARTICULAR

DUE TO COMMUNITY DEMAND, OUR SENSOR NETWORK KEPT EXPANDING ACROSS THE CITY.

EACH INSTALLATION TOOK A LOT OF WORK.

AND OLDER BUILDINGS, LIKE SRO HOTELS, WERE THE MOST DIFFICULT.

ACCESS POINTS WERE OFTEN NARROW AND TOUGH TO CLIMB.

GEEZ. DOESN'T LOOK THAT STURDY.

GIVEN THE RISK, I DIDN'T WANT TO ASK TOO MUCH OF COWORKERS.

BUT DANIELA KEPT UP WITH THE PACE.

AFTER MONTHS OF WORKING ALONE, THE COMPANY MADE FOR GOOD CONVERSATION.

HAVE YOU SEEN FRIENDS RECENTLY?

NOPE, HBOMAX RIGHT?

I READ IT'S JUST AN INTERVIEW WITH THE CAST, NOT AN ACTUAL NEW EPISODE.

OH, I DIDN'T MEAN FRIENDS, THE TV SHOW.

I MEANT FRIENDS...LIKE IN PERSON.

OH.

I REALIZED I DIDN'T NEED TO WORK ALONE ALL THE TIME.

WORKING WITH TEAMS OF DEDICATED COMMUNITY ORGANIZERS, ANALYSTS, AND VOLUNTEERS HELPED ME PUSH PAST BURNOUT.

DATA GAPS WERE FILLED IN FOR COMMUNITIES THAT COULDN'T AFFORD AIR QUALITY SENSORS.

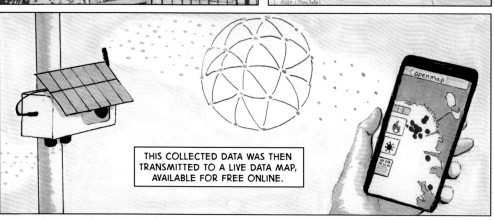

THIS COLLECTED DATA WAS THEN TRANSMITTED TO A LIVE DATA MAP, AVAILABLE FOR FREE ONLINE.

TO GET THE WORD OUT, WE PUT UP 500 POSTERS IN *SRO* BUILDINGS AND STOREFRONT WINDOWS.

TRANSLATING OUR MATERIALS INTO OTHER LANGUAGES HELPED REACH MORE COMMUNITIES.

WITH ALL THE IN-PERSON ORGANIZING, I DIDN'T THINK MUCH WORK COULD BE DONE THROUGH ZOOM.

PLUS, STARING AT ONE'S OWN FACE ALWAYS FELT WEIRD.

HRMM.

NEED A HAIRCUT AGAIN.

BUT HELP ARRIVED FROM AFAR IN UNEXPECTED WAYS.

STUDENTS AND PROFESSORS FROM STANFORD UNIVERSITY ASSISTED WITH AIR QUALITY DATA ANALYSIS...

...AND CREATED NEW EDUCATIONAL BOOKLETS ON AIR QUALITY SCIENCE.

AN ARMY OF ORGANIZERS THEN DISTRIBUTED THESE MATERIALS.

STUDENT LEADERS REPPING 10 HIGH SCHOOLS TABLED AT OUTDOOR FESTS AND MARKETS.

SURVEYS AND POSTERS WERE ALSO DISTRIBUTED BY 15 TENANT LEADERS FROM SRO BUILDINGS.

WITHIN WEEKS, WE GOT THE WORD OUT TO HUNDREDS OF RESIDENTS AND BUSINESSES.

SOCIAL DISTANCING DIDN'T MEAN THE END OF COMMUNITY.

IT'S IMPOSSIBLE TO KNOW WHAT MY GRANDFATHER WOULD HAVE THOUGHT OF ALL OF THIS.

MILITARY CONFLICT HAD SHAPED HIS UNDERSTANDING OF A FRONTLINE, PERHAPS ALSO REFLECTED IN THE TERSE PROSE OF HIS JOURNAL.

WITH MY OWN KOREAN LANGUAGE COMPREHENSION DECLINING FROM DISUSE, I WENT BACK AND STRUGGLED TO TRANSLATE MORE OF HIS JOURNAL.

THE FOOD DELIVERY, JOB TRAINING, AIR QUALITY MONITORING--IT WAS DIFFICULT TO MEASURE THIS WORK AGAINST HIS LIFE.

THE FRONTLINES OF TODAY WERE DIFFERENT AND CONSTANTLY SHIFTING.

163

ESPECIALLY AS **MORE** WAS DEMANDED OF WORKERS WHO DIDN'T EXPECT TO BE ON THE FRONTLINES THROUGHOUT 2020.

FROM GROCERS AND FARM WORKERS...

...TO WAREHOUSE EMPLOYEES AND THE POSTAL SERVICE...

...INFRASTRUCTURE AND INSTITUTIONS WERE PUT TO THE TEST.

JANUARY 6, 2021

INSTITUTIONS THAT TURNED OUT TO BE FAR MORE FRAGILE THAN EXPECTED.

AND AFTER THE CHAOS AND DAMAGE WERE DONE...

...**MORE** WAS ASKED OF FRONTLINE WORKERS TO PICK UP THE PIECES.

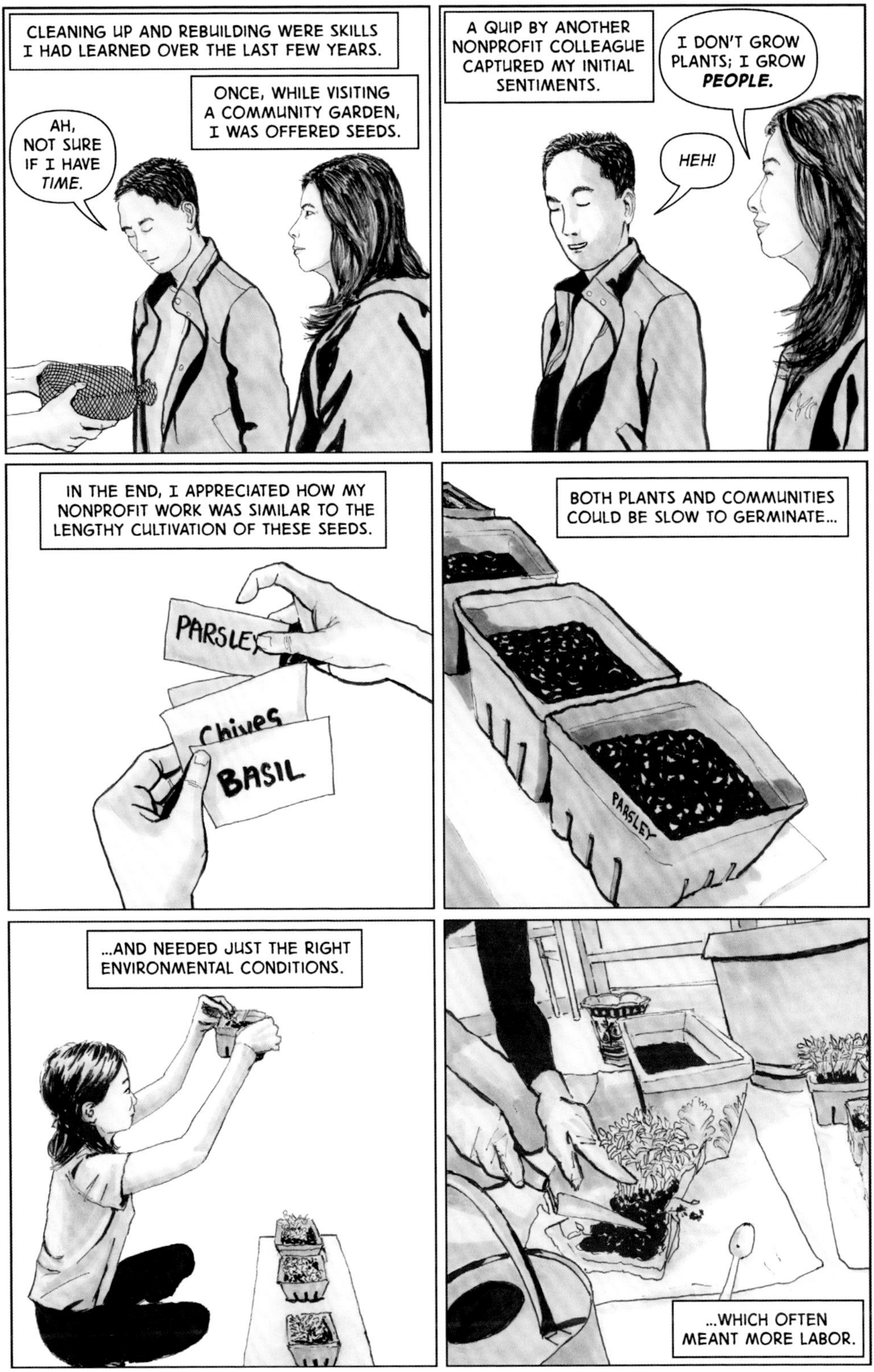
CLEANING UP AND REBUILDING WERE SKILLS I HAD LEARNED OVER THE LAST FEW YEARS.
ONCE, WHILE VISITING A COMMUNITY GARDEN, I WAS OFFERED SEEDS.
AH, NOT SURE IF I HAVE *TIME.*
A QUIP BY ANOTHER NONPROFIT COLLEAGUE CAPTURED MY INITIAL SENTIMENTS.
I DON'T GROW PLANTS; I GROW ***PEOPLE.***
HEH!
IN THE END, I APPRECIATED HOW MY NONPROFIT WORK WAS SIMILAR TO THE LENGTHY CULTIVATION OF THESE SEEDS.
PARSLEY
Chives
BASIL
BOTH PLANTS AND COMMUNITIES COULD BE SLOW TO GERMINATE...
PARSLEY
...AND NEEDED JUST THE RIGHT ENVIRONMENTAL CONDITIONS.
...WHICH OFTEN MEANT MORE LABOR.

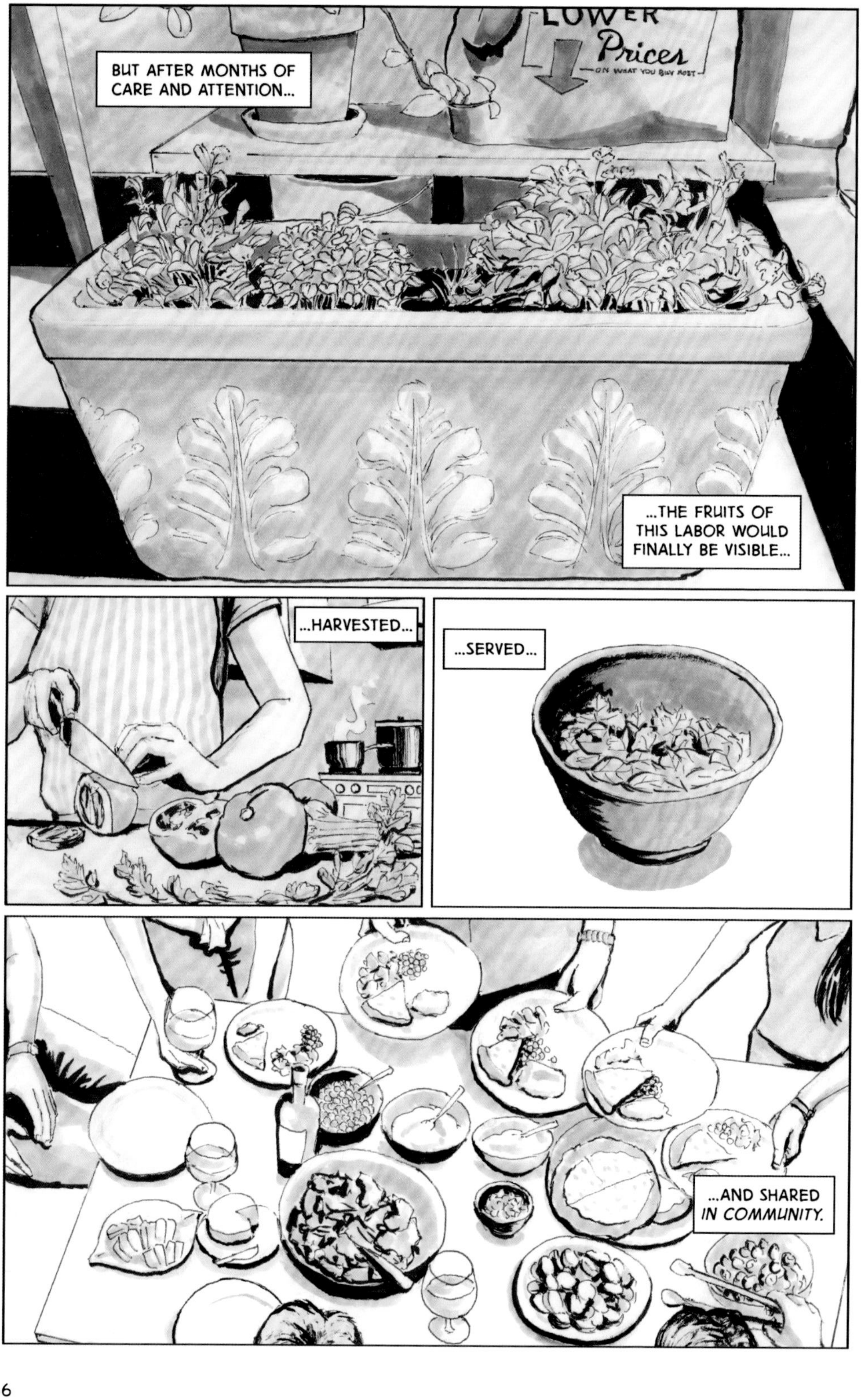
LOWER
Prices
BUT AFTER MONTHS OF CARE AND ATTENTION...
...THE FRUITS OF THIS LABOR WOULD FINALLY BE VISIBLE...
...HARVESTED...
...SERVED...
...AND SHARED *IN COMMUNITY.*

CHAPTER SEVEN

THE MORNING CALM

ON HIS LAST VISIT TO SAN FRANCISCO, MY DAD DOZED OFF A LOT.

Z Z Z

HE HAD ENJOYED MY ART INSTALLED ON UTILITY BOXES, AND I ALSO WANTED HIM TO BETTER UNDERSTAND MY WORK IN ENVIRONMENTAL POLICY.

IN ADDITION TO SERVING ON THE SAN FRANCISCO COMMISSION ON THE ENVIRONMENT, WHICH OVERSAW A CITY DEPARTMENT FOCUSED ON *LOCAL* POLICY, I HAD BEEN APPOINTED TO A NEW GOVERNMENT COMMISSION FOCUSED ON ***REGIONAL*** POLICIES FOR THE BAY AREA.

I DROVE HIM TO THE HQ FOR REGIONAL AGENCIES AND GENTLY PRODDED HIM AWAKE.

DAD, WE'RE HERE...TIME TO WAKE UP.

MY DAD NO LONGER WORE A LEATHER COAT, AND HE HAD BEEN DRESSING MORE LIKE A CHARACTER FROM *THE SOPRANOS*.

S BEALE STREET

ALTHOUGH HE NEVER SEEMED TO CARE TOO MUCH ABOUT GIFTS, I MADE A MENTAL NOTE TO TAKE HIM OUT TO ANOTHER NICE MEAL AFTER TOURING THE BUILDING.

HE AMBLED UP TO THE AIRY ENTRANCE, LINED WITH GLEAMING METALS, GLASS, AND REPURPOSED DOUGLAS FIR LOGS.

169

INSIDE THE BUILDING, MY DAD SURVEYED THE ROWS OF COMMISSIONER PHOTOS.

THE BAY CONSERVATION AND DEVELOPMENT COMMISSION (BCDC), THE NATION'S FIRST COASTAL ZONE AGENCY, HAD 27 REPRESENTATIVES.

MY DAD'S REACTION TO MY PHOTO WAS A BIT MUTED, MORE AMUSED THAN ANYTHING.

‹HUH, THERE'S EDDIE.›

Eddie Ahn
Speaker of the State Assembly Appointee

WHEN I LED TOURS OF THE BUILDING FOR HIGH SCHOOL YOUTH, THEY WERE EXCITED TO FIND A PERSONAL CONNECTION.

bcdc

IN CONTRAST, MY DAD WAS MORE IMPRESSED BY THE SIZE OF THE BUILDING.

‹WOW, THE CEILING IS SO HIGH!›

BUT HE REMAINED CONFUSED ABOUT THE ENVIRONMENTAL POLICIES AND AGENCIES LED BY COMMISSIONERS.

‹SO WHAT DO YOU DO NOW?›

‹IS THIS YOUR NEW FULL-TIME JOB?›

THE SHORT ANSWER WAS *NO,* MY ROLE ON *BCDC* WAS ONLY PART-TIME WORK.

I WAS THE RARE NONPROFIT WORKER APPOINTED AS A COMMISSIONER, SERVING WITH OTHER ELECTED OFFICIALS.

BCDC WAS CREATED FROM AN UNDERSTANDING THAT ENVIRONMENTAL IMPACTS IN THE BAY DIDN'T FOLLOW THE USUAL BOUNDARIES OF CITIES AND COUNTIES ACROSS THE REGION.

City A

County A

County B

City B

AS A STATE GOVERNMENT AGENCY WITH PERMITTING AND REGULATORY POWERS, *BCDC* BALANCED DIFFERENT PRIORITIES AND DEMANDS:

PUBLIC ACCESS TO THE BAY AND ENVIRONMENTAL CONSERVATION, AS WELL AS ECONOMIC DEVELOPMENT.

IN PUBLIC HEARINGS, COMMISSIONERS WOULD CONVENE TO WEIGH THESE PRIORITIES AS WELL AS VOTE ON PERMITS AND POLICIES THAT GUIDED THE AGENCY.

THE COMMISSION WOULD WORK WITH STAFF, SUCH AS PLANNERS, LAWYERS, AND SCIENTISTS WHO WERE FULL-TIME EMPLOYEES OF THE AGENCY.

AS A NONPROFIT ADVOCATE, I WAS USED TO SPEAKING AS A MEMBER OF THE PUBLIC FROM THIS SIDE OF THE PODIUM.

WHILE SITTING AND SPEAKING FROM THE *DAIS*, A RAISED PLATFORM OF THE HEARING ROOM, I BETTER UNDERSTOOD THE NUANCES OF MAKING POLICY...

...AND I REALIZED HOW HARD IT WAS TO MAKE GOOD DECISIONS, EVEN FROM A VANTAGE POINT OF BELIEVING IN CLIMATE CHANGE.

EDDIE AHN

INFORMATION WAS USUALLY LIMITED, AND BEST-AVAILABLE SCIENCE ONLY OFFERED A RANGE OF SCENARIOS.

WITHOUT BEING ABLE TO PREDICT THE FUTURE, IT WASN'T POSSIBLE TO MAKE *PERFECT* DECISIONS ABOUT CLIMATE ADAPTATION.

CLIMATE CHANGE ALSO SUPERCHARGED BIG SWINGS BETWEEN WET AND DRY PERIODS.

IN 2023, HEAVY RAINS IN CALIFORNIA FOLLOWED SEVERE DROUGHTS AND WILDFIRES.

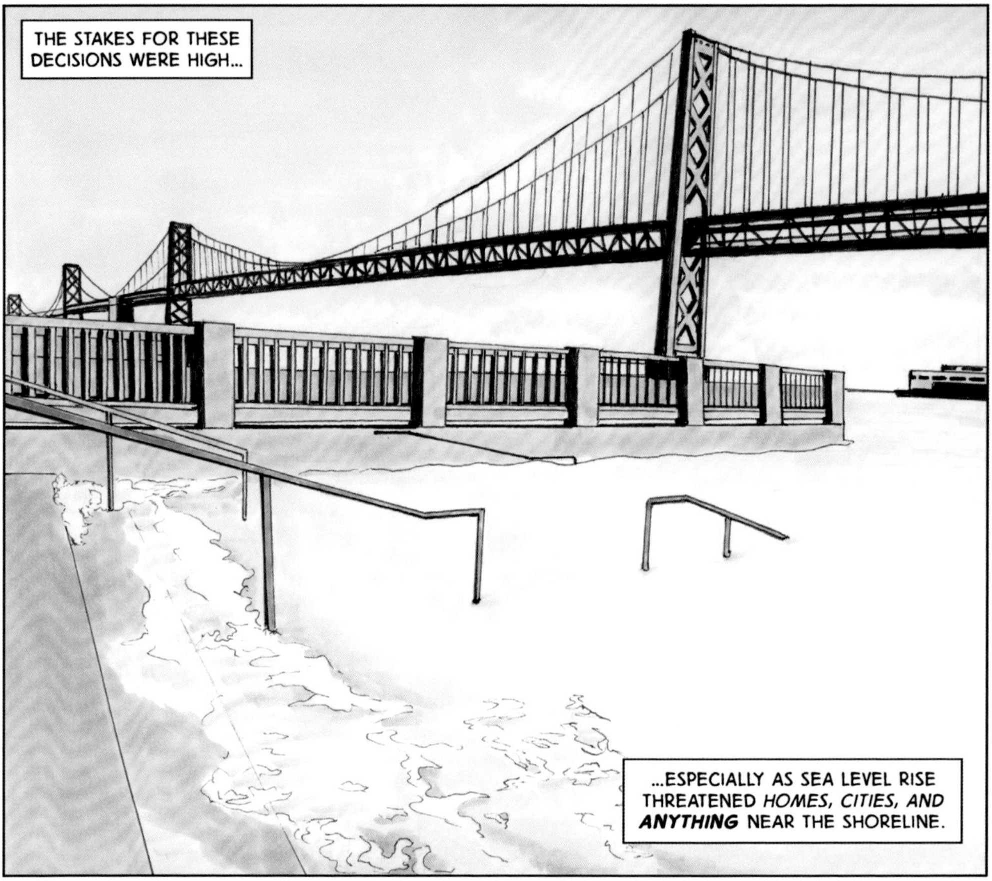
THE STAKES FOR THESE DECISIONS WERE HIGH...
...ESPECIALLY AS SEA LEVEL RISE THREATENED *HOMES, CITIES, AND* ***ANYTHING*** NEAR THE SHORELINE.

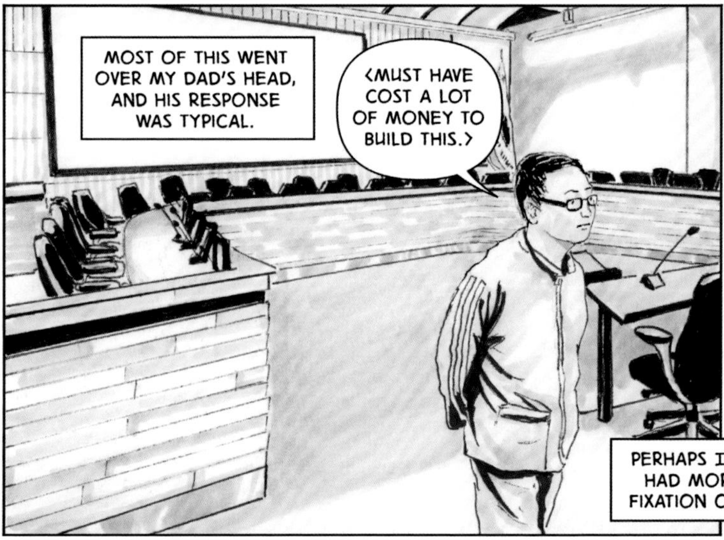
MOST OF THIS WENT OVER MY DAD'S HEAD, AND HIS RESPONSE WAS TYPICAL.
<MUST HAVE COST A LOT OF MONEY TO BUILD THIS.>
PERHAPS I SHOULD'VE HAD MORE OF HIS FIXATION ON MONEY...

...SINCE MY PERSONAL FINANCES WERE STILL IN DISARRAY.

THROUGHOUT 2022, MY CAR WAS BREAKING DOWN REPEATEDLY.

AND 13 YEARS AFTER STARTING NONPROFIT WORK, MY LAW SCHOOL LOANS WERE STILL LOOMING OVER ME.

DUE TO HIGH CALL VOLUMES, YOU MAY HAVE TO WAIT APPROXIMATELY 10 TO 15 MINUTES TO CONNECT TO A LOAN COUNSELOR.

PLEASE ACCEPT OUR APOLOGIES FOR THE DELAY.

IN THEORY, MY LOANS WERE SUPPOSED TO BE FORGIVEN AFTER 10 YEARS OF PUBLIC SERVICE.

AN HOUR LATER...

DUE TO HIGH CALL VOLUMES, YOU MAY HAVE TO WAIT APPROXIMATELY 10 TO 15 MINUTES TO CONNECT TO A LOAN COUNSELOR.

PLEASE ACCEPT OUR APOLOGIES FOR THE DELAY.

MRMM.

BUT PROBLEMS WITH THE PROGRAM HAD LED TO *YEARS* OF DELAYS...

...ADDING TO THE FEELING OF GOING NOWHERE FAST.

SARAH WAN HAD BEEN A NONPROFIT WORKER FOR DECADES, RISING FROM YOUTH COUNSELOR TO EXECUTIVE DIRECTOR OF A LARGE EDUCATION NONPROFIT. SHE KNEW MY WORK WELL, AND WE ALSO SERVED ON THE SF COMMISSION ON THE ENVIRONMENT TOGETHER SINCE 2017.

YOU'VE DONE GOOD WORK AT BRIGHTLINE, BUT IT'S HOLDING YOU BACK.

YOU'RE LIMITED BY BEING AT THAT NONPROFIT, AND I THINK YOU COULD BE DOING *MORE.*

THE COMMENT THAT I SHOULD BE DOING SOMETHING DIFFERENT WOULD REOCCUR...

...ESPECIALLY WITH PEOPLE WHO HAD KNOWN ME FOR LONGER. MY FRIENDS FROM POKER GAMES IN LAW SCHOOL WOULD ALSO WORRY FOR MY OWN SELF-INTEREST AND FUTURE.

OVER THE YEARS, THE DIFFERENT COMMUNITIES I'VE MET THROUGH YOU.

YOU'RE THE MOST *COMPLICATED* PERSON I KNOW.

WHILE I TOOK THIS AS A COMPLIMENT, I UNDERSTOOD ITS IMPLICIT CONCERN:

THAT I MIGHT BE EXERTING MYSELF *TOO MUCH* FOR OTHERS.

JANUARY 2022

STILL, I BELIEVED THAT BUILDING COMMUNITY WAS WORTH THE STRUGGLE.

I REMEMBERED THE TIME WHEN MY CAR'S MOTOR SUDDENLY GAVE OUT AS I TURNED A CORNER.

THE CAR COASTED TO THE EDGE OF *GEARY*, A BUSY STREET.

I CALLED A TOW TRUCK, BUT MOVING MY CAR OUT OF TRAFFIC NEEDED TO HAPPEN MORE QUICKLY.

AFTER PUTTING THE CAR IN NEUTRAL, I STRAINED TO MOVE IT, WITHOUT SUCCESS.

THIS LOOKED A *LOT* EASIER IN THE MOVIES.

A PARKING CONTROL OFFICER APPROACHED, AND I BRACED MYSELF, EXPECTING ANOTHER TICKET. INSTEAD, I GOT A SURPRISING OFFER.

NEED SOME HELP PUSHING?

174

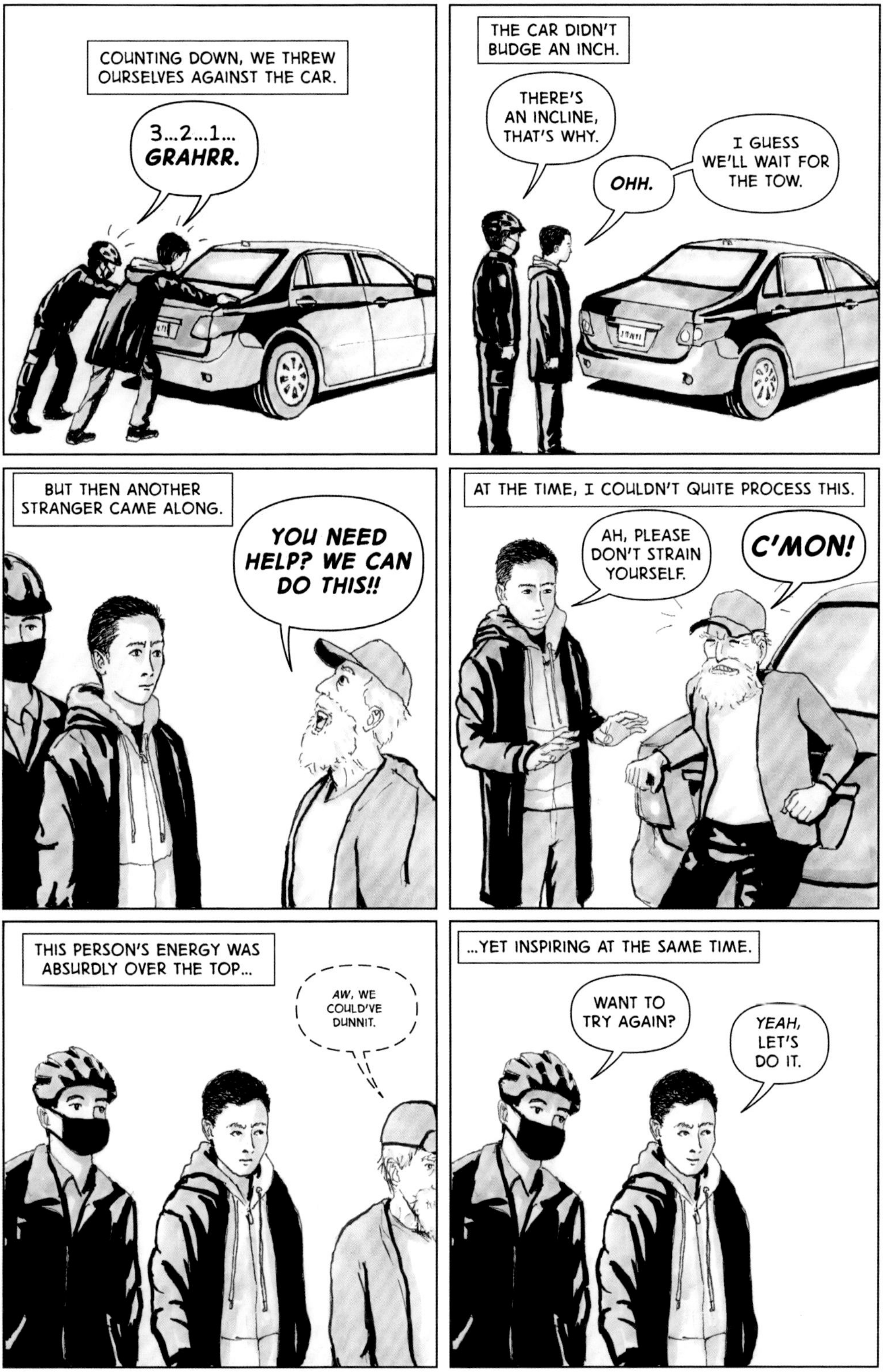
COUNTING DOWN, WE THREW OURSELVES AGAINST THE CAR.
3...2...1... GRAHRR.
THE CAR DIDN'T BUDGE AN INCH.
THERE'S AN INCLINE, THAT'S WHY.
OHH.
I GUESS WE'LL WAIT FOR THE TOW.
BUT THEN ANOTHER STRANGER CAME ALONG.
YOU NEED HELP? WE CAN DO THIS!!
AT THE TIME, I COULDN'T QUITE PROCESS THIS.
AH, PLEASE DON'T STRAIN YOURSELF.
C'MON!
THIS PERSON'S ENERGY WAS ABSURDLY OVER THE TOP...
AW, WE COULD'VE DUNNIT.
...YET INSPIRING AT THE SAME TIME.
WANT TO TRY AGAIN?
YEAH, LET'S DO IT.

WITHIN SECONDS, ANOTHER STRANGER CAME ALONG.

I'LL HELP--YOU GO PUSH AND STEER FROM THE FRONT.

3...2...1... GARGH! JUST GET IN!! STEER!!

GAINING MOMENTUM, THE CAR BEGAN TO GLIDE FORWARD.

UH, OK.

INITIALLY, I FELT UNCOMFORTABLE AND UNDESERVING OF ALL THIS.

THERE'S NO PARTICULAR REASON FOR **ANYONE** TO HELP IN THIS SITUATION.

BUT IN THE SPAN OF MINUTES, THREE STRANGERS HAD GONE OUT OF THEIR WAY.

TO THEM, I WAS JUST A RANDOM PERSON WITH A BROKEN-DOWN COROLLA.

PARTICULARLY WITH ALL THE CRAZY I'VE ENCOUNTERED SINCE THE PANDEMIC, I WAS SURPRISED TO COME ACROSS THIS MUCH GENEROSITY.

HOW YOU DOING UP THERE?

I ENJOYED THIS MOMENT FOR AS LONG AS IT LASTED.

ALL GOOD, THANKS.

APRIL 2022

THEN UNEXPECTED GOOD NEWS CAME OUT OF THE BLUE.

I FINALLY GOT A NOTICE CONFIRMING MY STUDENT LOANS WERE FORGIVEN.

AT FIRST, THE PUNCTUATION MADE ME SUSPICIOUS.

PUBLIC SERVICE LOAN FORGIVENESS UPDATE!

Account Number: 82 561

IN MY MIND, EXCLAMATIONS WERE USED FOR *WARNING NOTICES* AND *JUNKMAIL*.

AFTER 13 YEARS OF ENDLESS PAPERWORK AND PHONE CALLS, IT WAS HARD TO BELIEVE THIS WAS *IT*.

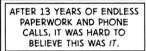

forgiven (Interest)	Oustanding Balance
38.45	$ 0.00
11.38	$ 0.00

no additional payments on these loans.

DOUBTFUL, I CALLED THE STUDENT LOAN SERVICER.

THERE'S REALLY NOTHING ELSE TO DO? NOTHING ELSE TO SIGN?

YES, BASED ON WHAT I'VE JUST PULLED UP, THERE'S NOTHING MORE FOR YOU TO DO...

brightline DEFENSE

...BUT HAVE A PARTY AND CELEBRATE.

HEHEHE HEHEHE

WELL...

...THANKS FOR SAYING SO.

WITH THIS BURDEN LIFTED, I FELT LIKE TIME ITSELF *SPED FORWARD.*

I WAS APPOINTED TO THE METROPOLITAN TRANSPORTATION COMMISSION (MTC), THE GOVERNMENT AGENCY THAT PLANNED AND FINANCED TRANSIT THROUGHOUT THE REGION.

AS A COMMISSIONER, I EVALUATED PROJECTS AND BUDGETS ON A VERY DIFFERENT SCALE...

...RANGING FROM OPERATING THE REGION'S BRIDGES...

Sonoma

Napa

Solano

Marin

Contra Costa

San Francisco

Alameda

San Mateo

Santa Clara

...TO FUNDING THE TRANSIT SYSTEMS THAT CONNECTED THE BAY AREA'S NINE COUNTIES AND 101 CITIES, SUCH AS HIGHWAYS, RAIL NETWORKS, SEAPORTS, AND AIRPORTS...

...AS WELL AS OVER TWO DOZEN LOCAL TRANSIT AGENCIES AND THE REGION'S FERRY SYSTEM.

MY NONPROFIT WORK WAS EXPANDING AS WELL.

I WAS QUICKLY LEARNING HOW TO BUILD A CLEAN ENERGY ECONOMY.

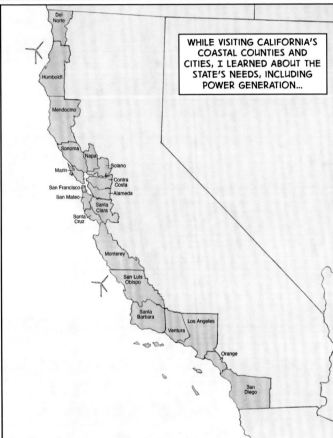

WHILE VISITING CALIFORNIA'S COASTAL COUNTIES AND CITIES, I LEARNED ABOUT THE STATE'S NEEDS, INCLUDING POWER GENERATION...

...TRANSMISSION AND ENERGY STORAGE...

...AND THE COMPLEXITY OF MANUFACTURING PROCESSES.

DON'T ASK ME QUESTIONS 'BOUT BLADES.

WE JUST BUILD THE BIG TUBE HERE!

SEPTEMBER 2022

KINCARDINE, SCOTLAND

IN LATE 2022, I TRAVELED ACROSS EUROPE TO KEEP EXPLORING NEWER CLEAN ENERGY TECHNOLOGIES.

FOR DEEP WATER DEPTHS, OFFSHORE WIND TURBINES COULD BE INSTALLED ON FLOATING SUBSTRUCTURES.

SIZING UP THIS WIND FARM, I WAS STRUCK BY HOW THE TURBINES WERE BOTH *LARGER* AND *SMALLER* THAN EXPECTED.

UP CLOSE, THE PROJECTS LOOMED *LARGE* IN SCALE, BUT THEY ALSO APPEARED *SMALL* AGAINST THE VASTNESS OF THE OCEAN...

...AND EVEN *SMALLER* AGAINST THE DESTRUCTION WROUGHT BY CLIMATE CHANGE.

SINCE ADDRESSING CLIMATE CHANGE NECESSITATED BIGGER SOLUTIONS ACROSS BORDERS AND DIFFERENT COMMUNITIES, MY WORK TRAVEL SCHEDULE *ACCELERATED.*

I WAS GOING TO AS MANY AS SEVEN STATES WITHIN A WEEK: NEW YORK, MASSACHUSETTS, RHODE ISLAND, PENNSYLVANIA, NEW JERSEY, WASHINGTON, AND CONNECTICUT...

...*PLUS* D.C. AND EVEN *MORE* TRAVEL ACROSS CALIFORNIA IN THE PRIOR WEEK.

I WOULD THEN RETURN TO MY NONPROFIT OFFICE AND STAFF, WHO WERE EXPANDING OUR PROGRAMS AND POLICY WORK.

ARE THOSE THE NEW AIR QUALITY SENSORS FROM UC BERKELEY?

YEAH, REPLACING THE BATTERY TAKES SOME PRACTICE.

EMERGING FROM THE PANDEMIC, THE OFFICE FELT VIBRANT AGAIN WITH NEW STAFF AND ACTIVITY.

AND THE ACCELERATION OF OUR WORK EVERY DAY FELT EXCITING.

WHAT'S UP WITH *ROCKY THE ROOMBA?*

VRMMM

I PUT GOOGLY EYES ON IT!

DO YOU LIKE IT?

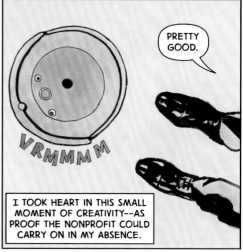

PRETTY GOOD.

VRMMMM

I TOOK HEART IN THIS SMALL MOMENT OF CREATIVITY—AS PROOF THE NONPROFIT COULD CARRY ON IN MY ABSENCE.

BUT JUST WHEN EVERYTHING SEEMED TO SETTLE INTO A GROOVE, FRESH CHALLENGES WOULD ARISE.

HUH, MY SISTER'S CALLING FROM ABROAD...

BZZT BZZT

AFTER PERMANENTLY MOVING TO SOUTH KOREA, MY DAD HAD BEGUN FORGETTING HIS ADDRESS.

HEY.

. . .

WHAT DO YOU MEAN, "HE CAN'T FIND HIS WAY HOME"?

HE WOULD THEN *WANDER,* SOMETIMES SLEEPING ON THE STREETS OVERNIGHT, UNTIL POLICE WOULD BRING HIM HOME.

ANOTHER BAD SIGN WAS THAT MY DAD WAS BECOMING INCREASINGLY IMPATIENT AND *BELLIGERENT* WITH DOCTORS AND MEDICAL STAFF.

SO STARTING IN OCTOBER 2022, I TRAVELED TO SEOUL MULTIPLE TIMES TO SEE MY DAD.

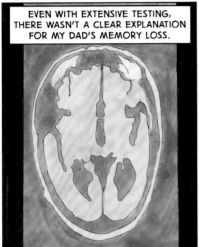

EVEN WITH EXTENSIVE TESTING, THERE WASN'T A CLEAR EXPLANATION FOR MY DAD'S MEMORY LOSS.

ONE THEORY WAS THAT EXCESS FLUID HAD BEEN BUILDING UP IN HIS SKULL AND PUTTING PRESSURE ON HIS BRAIN.

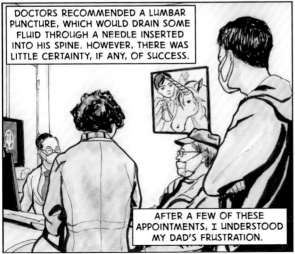

DOCTORS RECOMMENDED A LUMBAR PUNCTURE, WHICH WOULD DRAIN SOME FLUID THROUGH A NEEDLE INSERTED INTO HIS SPINE. HOWEVER, THERE WAS LITTLE CERTAINTY, IF ANY, OF SUCCESS.

AFTER A FEW OF THESE APPOINTMENTS, I UNDERSTOOD MY DAD'S FRUSTRATION.

THERE WERE NO MAGICAL SOLUTIONS... JUST A LONG SEARCH FOR THEM AHEAD.

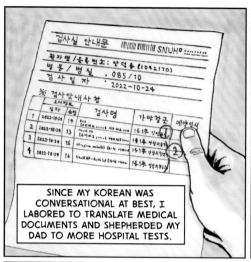

SINCE MY KOREAN WAS CONVERSATIONAL AT BEST, I LABORED TO TRANSLATE MEDICAL DOCUMENTS AND SHEPHERDED MY DAD TO MORE HOSPITAL TESTS.

AT LEAST HE WAS COMPLIANT WITH ME AROUND. HE WAITED PATIENTLY FOR COMPLEX SCANS...

...STRUGGLED THROUGH HIS MOBILITY TESTS...

...AND CHEERFULLY FAILED HIS MEMORY TESTS.

‹I'D LIKE YOU TO REMEMBER THREE WORDS FOR ME:›

‹AIRPLANE, PENCIL, PINETREE.›

‹CAN YOU REPEAT THE WORDS BACK TO ME?›

‹...THIS IS A TOUGH ONE.›

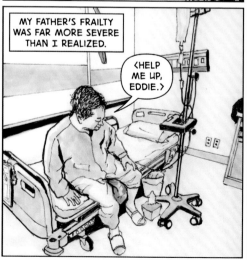

MY FATHER'S FRAILTY WAS FAR MORE SEVERE THAN I REALIZED.

‹HELP ME UP, EDDIE.›

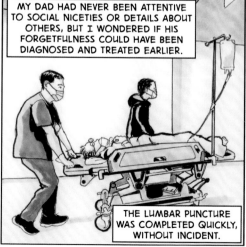

MY DAD HAD NEVER BEEN ATTENTIVE TO SOCIAL NICETIES OR DETAILS ABOUT OTHERS, BUT I WONDERED IF HIS FORGETFULNESS COULD HAVE BEEN DIAGNOSED AND TREATED EARLIER.

THE LUMBAR PUNCTURE WAS COMPLETED QUICKLY, WITHOUT INCIDENT.

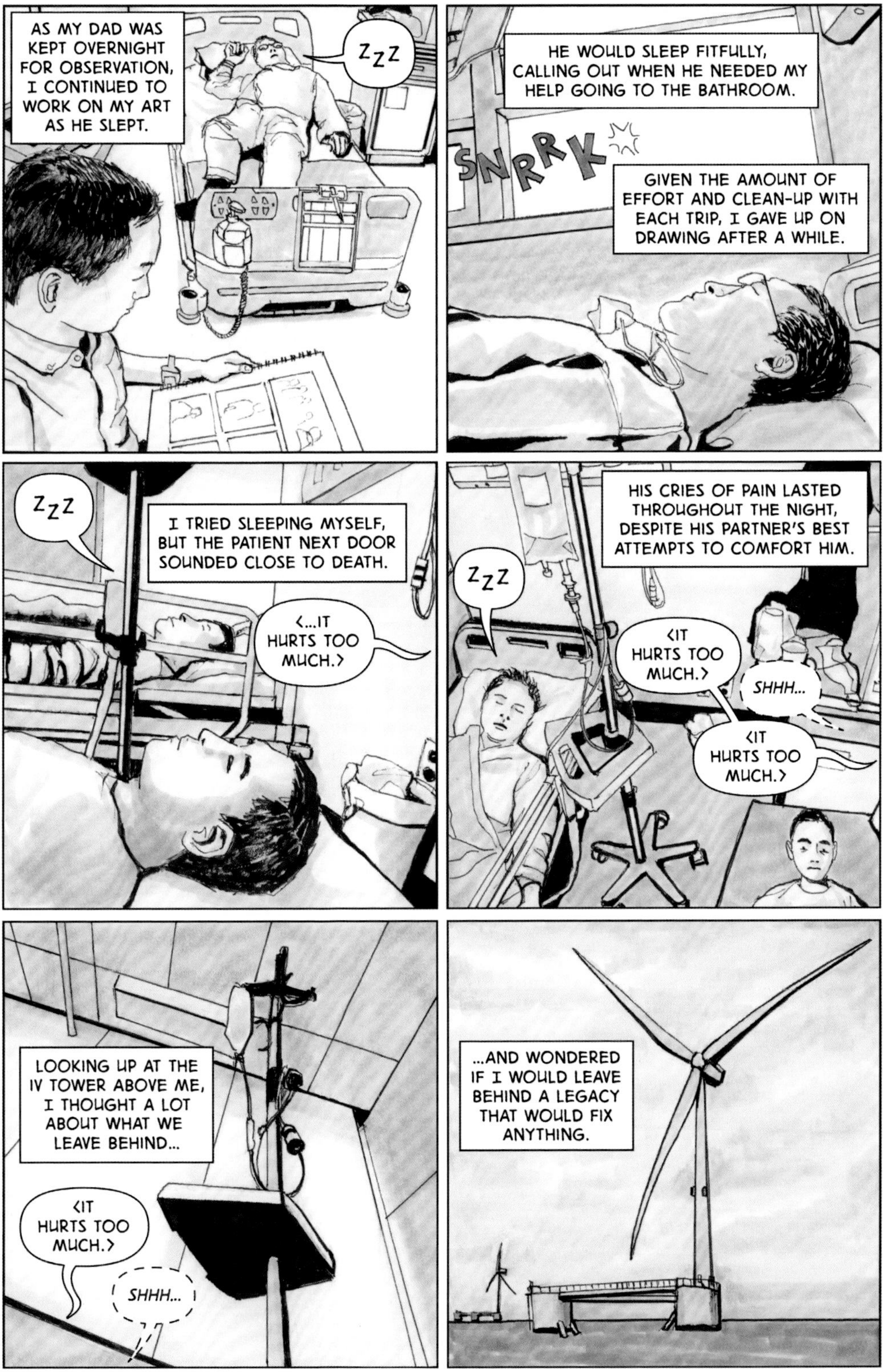

AS MY DAD WAS KEPT OVERNIGHT FOR OBSERVATION, I CONTINUED TO WORK ON MY ART AS HE SLEPT.
ZZZ
HE WOULD SLEEP FITFULLY, CALLING OUT WHEN HE NEEDED MY HELP GOING TO THE BATHROOM.
SNRRK
GIVEN THE AMOUNT OF EFFORT AND CLEAN-UP WITH EACH TRIP, I GAVE UP ON DRAWING AFTER A WHILE.
ZZZ
I TRIED SLEEPING MYSELF, BUT THE PATIENT NEXT DOOR SOUNDED CLOSE TO DEATH.
<...IT HURTS TOO MUCH.>
HIS CRIES OF PAIN LASTED THROUGHOUT THE NIGHT, DESPITE HIS PARTNER'S BEST ATTEMPTS TO COMFORT HIM.
ZZZ
<IT HURTS TOO MUCH.>
SHHH...
<IT HURTS TOO MUCH.>
LOOKING UP AT THE IV TOWER ABOVE ME, I THOUGHT A LOT ABOUT WHAT WE LEAVE BEHIND...
<IT HURTS TOO MUCH.>
SHHH...
...AND WONDERED IF I WOULD LEAVE BEHIND A LEGACY THAT WOULD FIX ANYTHING.

ALTHOUGH I DIDN'T FULFILL MY PARENTS' DREAMS FOR MY ECONOMIC MOBILITY, I DIDN'T DIVEST MYSELF FROM MY FAMILY'S HISTORY EITHER.

BEFORE VISITING MY DAD IN SOUTH KOREA, I HAD JUST TRAVELED TO DENMARK TO SEE MORE OFFSHORE WIND FARMS, AND I HAD A UNIQUE OPPORTUNITY TO SUIT UP FOR A HELICOPTER TOUR.

WE FLEW TO AN ACCOMMODATION PLATFORM, A LARGE STRUCTURE ON THE OCEAN THAT HOUSED MAINTENANCE PERSONNEL FOR THE WIND TURBINES.

WOW, WHAT A VIEW!

I WAS REMINDED OF MY DAD'S BALLOON RIDE BACK IN 1989.

TRYING TO MAKE CONVERSATION WITH MY DAD ONCE HE WAS AWAKE, I SHOWED HIM SOME PHOTOS OF MY HELICOPTER TRIP, BUT HE DIDN'T SEE THE CONNECTION.

‹AH, DON'T REMEMBER THAT.›

‹GO GET ME A COFFEE.›

WHEN I RETURNED WITH HIS COFFEE, MY DAD HAD RIPPED OUT HIS *IV* AND CLOTHED HIMSELF.

<WHAT'S GOING ON?>

<LET'S *GO*, EDDIE.>

HE STUMBLED TOWARD THE EXIT, AND I DID MY BEST TO CLEAN HIS TRAIL OF WASTE AND SPILLAGE.

WE WERE JOINED BY MY 92-YEAR-OLD PATERNAL GRANDMOTHER, WHO WAS INCREDIBLY SPRY AND HAD BEEN TAKING CARE OF MY FATHER.

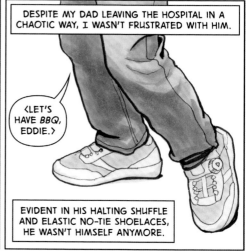

DESPITE MY DAD LEAVING THE HOSPITAL IN A CHAOTIC WAY, I WASN'T FRUSTRATED WITH HIM.

<LET'S HAVE *BBQ*, EDDIE.>

EVIDENT IN HIS HALTING SHUFFLE AND ELASTIC NO-TIE SHOELACES, HE WASN'T HIMSELF ANYMORE.

YET HE STILL WANTED TO TOUCH AND EXPERIENCE RANDOM THINGS AROUND HIM.

PLUCKING A FLOWER AS HE WALKED, HE INHALED ITS SCENT.

<SMELLS GOOD!>

I DIDN'T KNOW HE WAS CAPABLE OF THIS KIND OF SENTIMENTALITY.

THAT HE CARED ABOUT THE ENVIRONMENT *AT ALL* WAS SURPRISING.

WHEN WE SAT DOWN FOR LUNCH, MY DAD REVERTED TO HIS USUAL QUIRKS.

‹WHICH MEAT DO YOU WANT, DAD?›

‹THE MOST **EXPENSIVE** KIND.›

‹BECAUSE MY SON IS BUYING.›

‹CAN HE AFFORD IT? HAS HE SWITCHED JOBS?›

MY GRANDMOTHER HAD A VAGUE SENSE THAT I WAS A PUBLIC INTEREST ATTORNEY. I HAD DESCRIBED MY JOB TO MY DAD A DOZEN TIMES OVER THE YEARS, **BUT...**

‹...UH, I DON'T KNOW.›

‹WHAT DO YOU DO AGAIN, EDDIE?›

HIS SHEEPISH SMILE COULD HAVE BEEN HIS MEMORY LOSS...

...*OR THAT HE NEVER UNDERSTOOD MY LIFE IN THE FIRST PLACE. **EITHER** WAY, THE SACRIFICES AND COSTS OF MY WORK WERE NEVER HIS TO CARRY.*

INSTEAD, I FOCUSED ON THE HERE AND NOW.

‹HOW DOES IT TASTE?›

‹GOOD!›

AS WE ATE, IT WAS HARD TO IGNORE HIS VIOLENT COUGH, ANOTHER ONE OF HIS CHRONIC HEALTH ISSUES.

‹ARE YOU OK, DAD?›

hahkk!
hahkk!
hahkk!

WE STILL TRIED TO MAKE THE MOST OF THIS FINAL MEAL.

MMM!

WE TRIED WALKING HOME AFTER LUNCH.

THEN, MY DAD SAT DOWN ABRUPTLY. MY GRANDMOTHER KNEW WHAT THIS MEANT AND BEGAN LOOKING FOR A TAXI.

HIS MUSCLES WERE FAILING HIM, AND WITHOUT SPEAKING ANY WORDS, HE BEGAN TO SLOWLY FALL BACKWARD INTO THE BUSHES.

‹...IT'S TIME TO GO HOME.›

ALL THIS WAS ANOTHER REMINDER...

‹...OK.›

...THAT THERE'S ALWAYS A COST.

BETWEEN MY **NONPROFIT, GOVERNMENT COMMISSIONS,** AND **ART,** PERHAPS I HAD FOCUSED TOO MUCH ON WORK.

MY DAD NEVER REPROACHED ME FOR NOT VISITING HIM ENOUGH, BUT I KNEW HIS HEALTH WOULD LIKELY LIMIT OUR TIME TOGETHER...

...AND I THOUGHT A LOT ABOUT TIME AS THE *ENEMY.*

OVER THE YEARS, MY UTILITY BOX ART IN SAN FRANCISCO HAS WEATHERED A LOT...

...BAKING HEATWAVES AND PERIODS OF DROUGHT...

...ASH FROM WILDFIRES...

...INTENSE RAINSTORMS AND "BOMB CYCLONES"...

...AND GRAFFITI.

WHILE THIS ART HAS BEEN OK AFTER EXTREME CLIMATE CHANGE EVENTS, IT DID NEED A CLEANING WHEN OCCASIONALLY TAGGED.

I DIDN'T MIND THE EXTRA WORK...

...ESPECIALLY WHEN I THOUGHT ABOUT MY DAD'S PAST APPRECIATION FOR MY ART...

...AND HOW HIS SENTIMENTALITY MIGHT ENDURE IN SURPRISING WAYS.

NEXT TO THESE BOXES, STRANGERS HAVE CONTRIBUTED FLOWERS...

...AND CAREFULLY WRAPPED THEM TO PROTECT AGAINST CONSTRUCTION DUST.

IT'S REALLY NO ONE'S *JOB* TO TAKE CARE OF THESE BOXES...

...BUT THERE'S STILL A COMMUNITY THAT HAS CARED FOR THEM.

SO IN THAT SPIRIT, I *KEEP ON* KEEPING ON.

AND I'D LIKE TO THINK IF MY DAD EVER COMES BACK...

...HE WOULD UNDERSTAND.

A FEW MONTHS LATER, WHILE DRAWING WITH MY NIECE, EDIE, I BECAME MORE AWARE OF GETTING OLDER.

IT WAS FUN TO SEE MY ART WITH A FRESH PERSPECTIVE.

AS EDIE UNCAPPED A WHITEOUT PEN, I WAS REMINDED TO DRAW MYSELF WITH MORE WHITE HAIR.

IT WAS ALSO A WHILE SINCE A STRANGER HAD DEMANDED RANDOM SERVICES FROM ME.

MAYBE WITH AGE, I DIDN'T ATTRACT THAT KIND OF ATTENTION ANYMORE.

ON THE ONE HAND, IT WAS NICE TO AVOID WEIRD IMPOSITIONS. ON THE OTHER, I WONDERED IF I SHOULD HAVE BEEN WORRIED ABOUT LOSING MY YOUTH.

BUT THEN, AS I WAITED FOR TAKEOUT IN A RESTAURANT:

WHERE DO I PICK UP MY ORDER?

SORRY, DON'T WORK HERE.

OH, OK.

WELP... **STILL** GOT IT.

I *HAD* TO FIND SMALL MOMENTS OF JOY WHENEVER I COULD.

SINCE MY CHILDHOOD, SMALL MOMENTS OF JOY DEFINED OUR FAMILY, LIKE THE TIME WE FED PIGEONS WITH LEFTOVER MOVIE POPCORN.

MY MATERNAL GRANDMOTHER HELPED MY SISTER AND ME.

MY DAD JUST WATCHED, MAKING ODD COMMENTS TO HIMSELF.

THEY MUST BE HUNGRY!

AND MY GRANDFATHER LOOKED AS ALOOF AS EVER.

DECADES LATER, IT WAS CLEAR THE GAP BETWEEN MY MOM AND GRANDFATHER PERSISTED AS WE PORED OVER HIS PAPERS.

HMPH.

SHE REFUSED TO GO OVER SOME SECTIONS WITH ME.

‹I DON'T REALLY LIKE THIS PAGE.›

AND TRANSLATED OTHERS.

‹HE NOTES *HERE* THAT HIS WIFE WENT...›

"TO THE COMMUNITY CENTER."

‹THERE ARE TOO MANY PAGES OF THIS.›

‹YOUR GRANDFATHER WOULD RECORD ALL THE COMINGS AND GOINGS OF HIS WIFE AS WELL AS OTHER FAMILY MEMBERS.›

‹WHILE HE JUST STAYED AT HOME.›

‹ALONE.›

‹*WHO* DOES THAT?›

WHO *DOES* THAT?

AS MY MOM SLIPPED INTO SPEAKING ENGLISH AGAIN, I COULD SEE YEARS OF RESENTMENT FLASH ACROSS HER FACE.

...HE WAS SO *LONELY*.

SENSING SHE NEEDED SPACE, I LET MY MOM BE AS SHE WALKED AWAY.

MY GRANDFATHER'S MOTIVES WERE TOO PAINFUL TO EXPLAIN.

THE MOST GENEROUS INTERPRETATION OF MY GRANDFATHER WAS THAT HE WAS A PATRIOTIC IDEALIST AND UNCOMPROMISING IN HIS INTEGRITY AND GENEROSITY.

A LESS CHARITABLE ONE WAS THAT IN SERVICE TO HIS OWN DREAMS AND LACKING ACUMEN, HE FAILED TO TAKE CARE OF HIS OWN FAMILY.

IN THE LATTER EXPLANATION, I SAW THE UNCOMFORTABLE PARALLELS WITH MY OWN CHOICES.

WAS MY OWN LIFE TO END WITH THE SAME RESENTMENTS FROM MY OWN FAMILY?

WAS I SACRIFICING *TOO MUCH* FOR *TOO LITTLE*?

THE SUM OF MY LIFE ALSO TO BE REDUCED TO DUSTY PAPERS AND SOME PHOTOGRAPHS.

I REMEMBER A SPECIFIC MOMENT IN 2020 AS WILDFIRES WERE SCORCHING THE SKIES...

...I WAS SUPPORTING A JOB TRAINING PROGRAM AND NEVER WENT INTO MUCH DETAIL ABOUT THE SCOPE OF MY WORK AND LIFE WITH TRAINEES.

OH, SURE. I WORK FOR A NONPROFIT.

BUT ONCE, THERE WAS AN UNEXPECTED RESPONSE FROM A GRADUATE OF OUR JOB TRAINING PROGRAM:

I FEEL **BAD** FOR YOU, MAN.

WORKING THAT HARD, NOT GETTING PAID...

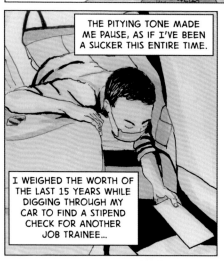

THE PITYING TONE MADE ME PAUSE, AS IF I'VE BEEN A SUCKER THIS ENTIRE TIME.

I WEIGHED THE WORTH OF THE LAST 15 YEARS WHILE DIGGING THROUGH MY CAR TO FIND A STIPEND CHECK FOR ANOTHER JOB TRAINEE...

...AND AS IF READING MY MIND, HE SAID:

...I HOPE YOU KNOW, EDDIE.

WE APPRECIATE EVERYTHING YOU DO.

I WAS TAKEN ABACK AND UNSURE HOW TO RESPOND.

EVEN THOUGH I LOOKED TIRED, THANKS OR VALIDATION WEREN'T NEEDED. I'M JUST MEETING THE COMMUNITY WHERE THEY'RE AT.

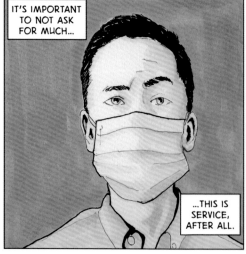

IT'S IMPORTANT TO NOT ASK FOR MUCH...

...THIS IS SERVICE, AFTER ALL.

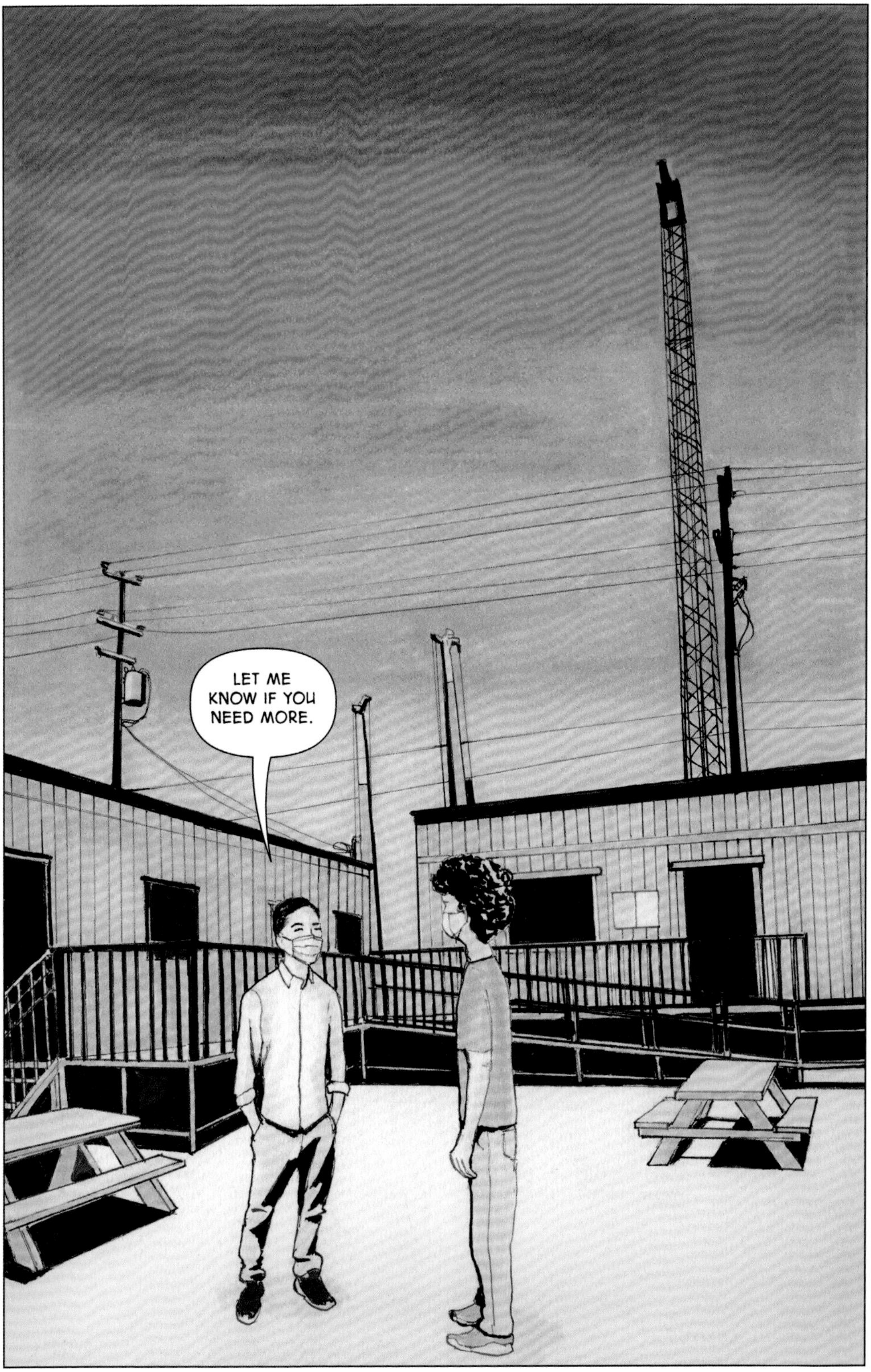
LET ME KNOW IF YOU NEED MORE.

THE JOURNEY TO CREATING *ADVOCATE*

AS MENTIONED EARLIER IN THIS BOOK, MY ART HAS BEEN DEVELOPED OVER A VERY LONG PERIOD OF TIME.

MY INTEREST IN CARTOONING BEGAN WITH THE COMIC STRIP FORMAT. I COMPILED MY EARLIEST WORK INTO BOOKLETS, OR ZINES, AFTER RECOVERING FROM EYE SURGERY.

IN ONE COMIC STRIP, I CREATED A SURLY, TALKING TURTLE NAMED *TEE* THAT RAN A COFFEE CART IN THE AVENUES, WHICH IS A NICKNAME FOR WESTERN SAN FRANCISCO.

booklet no. 1

THE TURTLE CHARACTER ITSELF WAS LOOSELY INSPIRED BY MY GRANDFATHER'S PERSONALITY BUT HEAVILY FICTIONALIZED FOR THE PURPOSES OF THE NARRATIVE.

THESE COMICS WERE LATER PUBLISHED IN *HYPHEN MAGAZINE*, A NONPROFIT NEWS AND CULTURE MAGAZINE THAT HIGHLIGHTED THE STORIES OF ASIAN AMERICANS. MY FIRST SOLO ART SHOW ALSO DOUBLED AS A FUNDRAISER FOR *HYPHEN*, AND I ENJOYED ORGANIZING MORE SOLO ART SHOWS OVER THE YEARS.

MY LAW PROFESSOR JOHN DIAMOND AND HIS PARTNER, LUCIA, AT ONE OF MY ART SHOWS IN SAN FRANCISCO. THESE SHOWS WOULD GATHER 100 TO 300 PEOPLE AT A TIME.

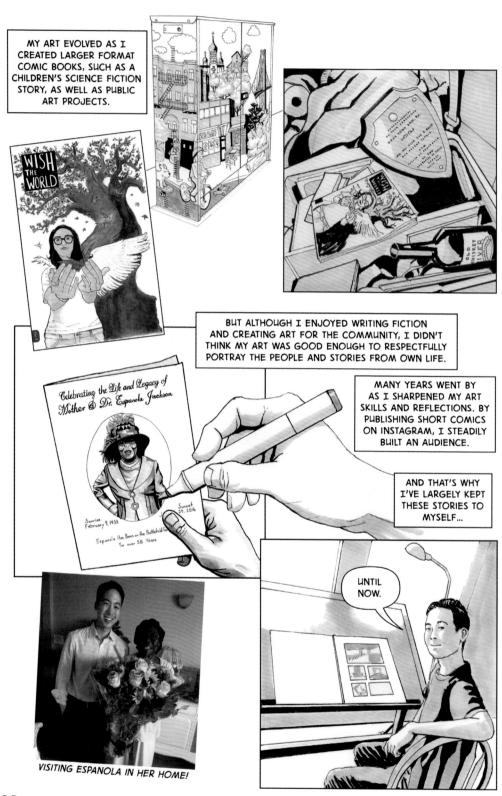

MY ART EVOLVED AS I CREATED LARGER FORMAT COMIC BOOKS, SUCH AS A CHILDREN'S SCIENCE FICTION STORY, AS WELL AS PUBLIC ART PROJECTS.

WISH THE WORLD

BUT ALTHOUGH I ENJOYED WRITING FICTION AND CREATING ART FOR THE COMMUNITY, I DIDN'T THINK MY ART WAS GOOD ENOUGH TO RESPECTFULLY PORTRAY THE PEOPLE AND STORIES FROM OWN LIFE.

MANY YEARS WENT BY AS I SHARPENED MY ART SKILLS AND REFLECTIONS. BY PUBLISHING SHORT COMICS ON INSTAGRAM, I STEADILY BUILT AN AUDIENCE.

AND THAT'S WHY I'VE LARGELY KEPT THESE STORIES TO MYSELF...

Celebrating the Life and Legacy of Mother & Dr. Espanola Jackson

Sunrise February 9, 1933

Sunset 29, 2016

Espanola Has Been on the Battlefield for For over 58 Years

UNTIL NOW.

VISITING ESPANOLA IN HER HOME!

ADVOCATING FOR ENVIRONMENTAL JUSTICE...

THE FIGHT FOR ENVIRONMENTAL JUSTICE IS ABOUT ADDRESSING POLLUTION AND HEALTH IMPACTS IN LOW-INCOME AND MARGINALIZED COMMUNITIES.

"SAVING THE PLANET" HAS BEEN A TRADITIONAL FRAME OF THE ENVIRONMENTAL MOVEMENT, BUT *ENVIRONMENTAL JUSTICE* FOCUSES ON COMMUNITY NEEDS AS WELL AS ECONOMIC EQUITY AND THE ENVIRONMENT.

THIS MULTIFACETED APPROACH TO CLIMATE CHANGE ACTION IS WHY I'VE WORKED ON THE WIDE RANGE OF PROJECTS PORTRAYED IN THIS BOOK, FROM *CLEAN ENERGY POLICY* TO A *JOB TRAINING PROGRAM FOR AT-RISK YOUTH.*

A COMMUNITY MEETING ABOUT THEIR NEEDS AND AIR QUALITY MONITORING, WHICH LATER LED TO SITING AIR QUALITY SENSORS IN 2020.

I ALSO CONSTANTLY THINK ABOUT THE *COSTS AND TRADE-OFFS* IN MY WORK, SUCH AS THE EMISSIONS IN MY WORK TRAVEL. DURING THE PANDEMIC, I DELIVERED 1,300 MEALS TO LOW-INCOME TENANTS, BUT HOW DOES THE SOCIAL VALUE OF THAT WORK WEIGH AGAINST THE ENVIRONMENTAL COSTS OF USING MY CAR?

DESPITE THE IMPERFECTIONS IN THIS INDIVIDUAL CARBON FOOTPRINT, I BELIEVE IN MY WORK'S VALUE IN ADDRESSING CLIMATE CHANGE THAT DEVASTATES EVERYONE'S QUALITY OF LIFE AND INFLICTS WIDESPREAD ECONOMIC DAMAGE.

THE REPORT ESTIMATES ADAPTING TO SEA LEVEL RISE WILL COST $110 BILLION...

...BUT THE PARTIAL COST OF INACTION IS *WORSE*...

OVER *$230* BILLION.

GEEZ, THAT'S A LOT OF BURRITOS.

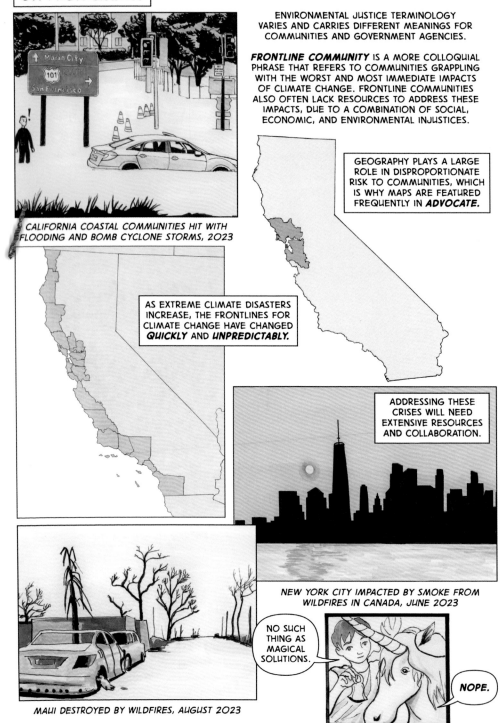

ON FRONTLINES...

CALIFORNIA COASTAL COMMUNITIES HIT WITH FLOODING AND BOMB CYCLONE STORMS, 2023

ENVIRONMENTAL JUSTICE TERMINOLOGY VARIES AND CARRIES DIFFERENT MEANINGS FOR COMMUNITIES AND GOVERNMENT AGENCIES.

FRONTLINE COMMUNITY IS A MORE COLLOQUIAL PHRASE THAT REFERS TO COMMUNITIES GRAPPLING WITH THE WORST AND MOST IMMEDIATE IMPACTS OF CLIMATE CHANGE. FRONTLINE COMMUNITIES ALSO OFTEN LACK RESOURCES TO ADDRESS THESE IMPACTS, DUE TO A COMBINATION OF SOCIAL, ECONOMIC, AND ENVIRONMENTAL INJUSTICES.

GEOGRAPHY PLAYS A LARGE ROLE IN DISPROPORTIONATE RISK TO COMMUNITIES, WHICH IS WHY MAPS ARE FEATURED FREQUENTLY IN *ADVOCATE.*

AS EXTREME CLIMATE DISASTERS INCREASE, THE FRONTLINES FOR CLIMATE CHANGE HAVE CHANGED *QUICKLY* AND *UNPREDICTABLY.*

ADDRESSING THESE CRISES WILL NEED EXTENSIVE RESOURCES AND COLLABORATION.

NEW YORK CITY IMPACTED BY SMOKE FROM WILDFIRES IN CANADA, JUNE 2023

MAUI DESTROYED BY WILDFIRES, AUGUST 2023

NO SUCH THING AS MAGICAL SOLUTIONS.

NOPE.

ADVOCATING FOR ONESELF...

I THOUGHT CAREFULLY ABOUT THIS BOOK'S INCLUSION OF RACIAL SLURS, AND I'VE WORRIED THAT RETELLING THESE STORIES GRANTS THEM MORE STAYING POWER IN MY OWN LIFE.

BUT AS THIS BOOK IS ABOUT LIVED EXPERIENCES, IT WAS IMPORTANT TO PORTRAY THE EVERYDAY CHALLENGES OF ASSERTING ONE'S RIGHT TO DIGNITY IN AMERICA.

SADLY, THIS BOOK DOES *NOT* COMPREHENSIVELY DETAIL ALL THE RACIAL SLURS IN MY LIFE, AND I'VE ALSO NEVER THOUGHT MY STORIES WERE ESPECIALLY UNIQUE, EVEN BEFORE ANTI-ASIAN HATE BURST INTO PUBLIC VIEW IN 2022.

WHILE THESE INCIDENTS HAVE MOTIVATED MY SERVICE IN BRIDGING COMMUNITIES, THEIR FREQUENCY AND REOCCURENCE IN RECENT YEARS HAVE MADE ME WONDER IF MY NONPROFIT WORK HAS BEEN *ENOUGH.*

WHEN THESE THOUGHTS COME UP, I REMIND MYSELF THAT THERE'S NEVER A CLEARLY DEFINED VICTORY THAT DEFEATS INJUSTICE ONCE AND FOR ALL, UNLIKE THE SWEEPING CONFLICTS AND RESOLUTIONS IN SUPERHERO MOVIES. MOREOVER, I'VE SEEN THE SMALL DETAILS OF MY WORK MAKE A DIFFERENCE AND BRING POSITIVE CHANGE TO THE COMMUNITIES I WORK WITH. IT'S THE SMALL VICTORIES THAT COUNT AND GIVE ME THE RESILIENCE TO CONTINUE MY ADVOCACY.

CLEANING UP BOX ART IN SAN FRANCISCO, 2023

CREATING THIS BOOK HAS HELPED ME THINK THROUGH AND STRIKE A BETTER BALANCE IN ADVOCATING FOR MYSELF TOO.

THANK YOU FOR JOINING ME ON THIS JOURNEY.

ACKNOWLEDGMENTS

THE STORY OF THIS BOOK'S CREATION IS VERY MUCH A ROLLERCOASTER FULL OF TWISTS AND TURNS IN ITS ROAD TO PUBLICATION. AFTER YEARS OF HONING THE GRAPHIC STORYTELLING STYLE OF *ADVOCATE*, I BEGAN TO POST THESE PAGES AS SHORT COMIC STORIES ON SOCIAL MEDIA IN EARLY 2020. MUCH OF THE CREDIT FOR WHAT YOU HOLD IN YOUR HANDS GOES TO MY EDITOR, VEDIKA KHANNA, WHO DISCOVERED AND IDENTIFIED ITS EARLY POTENTIAL AND THEN NURTURED THE CREATIVE VISION INTO A LARGER BOOK. OVER THE YEARS, MY AGENT, CHAD LUIBL, HAS BEEN AN ESSENTIAL PARTNER AND GUIDED THIS BOOK TO THE FINISH LINE.

A LARGER COMMUNITY HAS ALSO PITCHED IN FOR THE PRODUCTION OF THIS BOOK. MY FRIENDS EDDI CHANG AND EDWIN CHANG TRANSLATED MANY PAGES OF OLDER HISTORICAL DOCUMENTS THAT SHAPED ADVOCATE. THIS BOOK WAS ALSO HONED WITH EDITS AND CREATIVE INPUT FROM ONE OF THE MOST GIFTED ARTISTS THAT I KNOW, HAAN LEE, AS WELL AS ROMA PANGANIBAN OF JANKLOW & NESBIT ASSOCIATES. GENEROUSLY PROVIDING ARTISTIC GUIDANCE AND EXPERTISE EARLY ON, VALERIE LI AND KIRBY KIM DESERVE SPECIAL THANKS FOR PUTTING THIS BOOK ON TRACK WHEN THE PROGRESS TOWARD PUBLICATION COULD HAVE STALLED.

CREDIT FOR KEY ASPECTS OF BOOK DESIGN GOES TO BRIAN WONG, ALONG WITH THE EXCELLENT GRAPHIC DESIGN TEAM OF TEN SPEED GRAPHIC, CHLOE RAWLINS AND MEGGIE RAMM. A LARGER TEAM AT TEN SPEED GRAPHIC HAS ALSO SHAPED AND PROMOTED THIS BOOK, INCLUDING SOHAYLA FARMAN, DAN MYERS, CLAIRE LEONARD, MAYA BRADFORD, PAOLA CRESPO, KAITLIN KETCHUM, AND AARON WEHNER.

GIVEN THE BREADTH OF MY NONPROFIT WORK, I RECOGNIZE THERE ARE MANY, MANY DEDICATED STAFF AND VOLUNTEERS AS WELL AS COMMUNITY MEMBERS AND LEADERS THAT WERE NOT NAMED AND ILLUSTRATED IN THIS BOOK. I AM ALSO LUCKY TO HAVE DOZENS OF FRIENDS IN MY LIFE, WHO HAVE ALLOWED ME THE SPACE AND TIME TO CREATE THIS WORK.

OF COURSE, MY FAMILY HAS BEEN SUPPORTIVE OF THIS ENDEAVOR--MY WORK HAS BEEN ALWAYS HARD TO UNDERSTAND, BUT THEIR SACRIFICES FOR MY EDUCATION AND PATIENCE WITH MY LIFE LED TO WHAT IS THE CULMINATION OF THOUSANDS OF DRAWING HOURS. FINALLY, SPECIAL THANKS TO ANNY, MY EDITOR IN CHIEF--WITHOUT HER PATIENCE AND SUPPORT THIS BOOK WOULD NEVER HAVE BEEN COMPLETED.

ABOUT THE AUTHOR

VALENTINA SADIUL

EDDIE AHN HAS BEEN AN ENVIRONMENTAL JUSTICE ATTORNEY AND NONPROFIT WORKER FOR 15 YEARS. WHILE WORKING AS THE EXECUTIVE DIRECTOR OF BRIGHTLINE DEFENSE, A SAN FRANCISCO-BASED ENVIRONMENTAL JUSTICE NONPROFIT, HE WAS INDUCTED INTO THE STATE OF CALIFORNIA'S CLEAN ENERGY HALL OF FAME FOR HIS WORK IN EQUITY AND CLEAN ENERGY. IN ADDITION TO HIS NONPROFIT WORK, HE HAS SERVED AS PRESIDENT OF THE SAN FRANCISCO COMMISSION ON THE ENVIRONMENT AS WELL AS A COMMISSIONER ON THE METROPOLITAN TRANSPORTATION COMMISSION AND BAY CONSERVATION AND DEVELOPMENT COMMISSION. HE IS A SELF-TAUGHT ARTIST WHO HAS BEEN RECOGNIZED AS A CARTOONIST-IN-RESIDENCE BY THE CHARLES M. SCHULZ MUSEUM IN SANTA ROSA, CALIFORNIA.

PUBLISHED IN THE UNITED STATES BY TEN SPEED GRAPHIC,
AN IMPRINT OF THE CROWN PUBLISHING GROUP, A DIVISION
OF PENGUIN RANDOM HOUSE LLC, NEW YORK.
TENSPEED.COM

TEN SPEED GRAPHIC AND COLOPHON ARE TRADEMARKS
OF PENGUIN RANDOM HOUSE LLC.

TYPEFACE: BLAMBOT'S DIGITALSTRIP 2 AND HANODED'S
BRUSH CRUSH

LIBRARY OF CONGRESS CATALOGING-IN-PUBLICATION DATA
IS ON FILE WITH THE PUBLISHER.
LIBRARY OF CONGRESS CONTROL NUMBER: 2023949258

HARDCOVER ISBN: 978-1-9848-6249-5
EBOOK ISBN: 978-1-9848-6250-1

PRINTED IN CHINA

EDITOR: VEDIKA KHANNA
PRODUCTION EDITOR: SOHAYLA FARMAN
EDITORIAL ASSISTANT: KAUSAUR FAHIMUDDIN
ART DIRECTOR AND DESIGNER: CHLOE RAWLINS
COVER CO-DESIGNER: MEGGIE RAMM
COLORIST AND LETTERER: EDDIE AHN
PRODUCTION MANAGER: DAN MYERS
COPYEDITOR: KATE BOLEN
PROOFREADER: MIKAYLA BUTCHART
PUBLICIST: MAYA BRADFORD
MARKETER: PAOLA CRESPO

10 9 8 7 6 5 4 3 2 1

FIRST EDITION